My Life Beyond
LEUKEMIA

A Mayo Clinic patient story
by Hey Gee and Rae Burremo

Foreword

When I was five and a half years old, my legs started to hurt so much that I couldn't walk. My parents took me to the doctor. After a couple weeks, we figured out that the pain was being caused by cancer in my blood called acute lymphoblastic leukemia.

My life changed a lot after that. I had to take medicine at home and go to the hospital to get more medicine called **chemotherapy**. The **chemotherapy** was put into my blood through a **port** and into my spinal column. The medicine made me better, but it made me feel bad. It made me lose all my hair, too. Sometimes I wore a wig or a headscarf, but it grew back after a while. The **chemotherapy** medicine also made my **immune system** weak, so it was hard to fight off sickness and sometimes I had to stay away from my friends and siblings to protect myself from germs. That was really hard.

Now that I'm done with treatment and I'm cancer-free, I wanted to tell my story so other kids can understand a little more about what it's like to have leukemia.

Rae Burremo

"

REMAIN THE MASTER OF YOUR OWN BODY

"

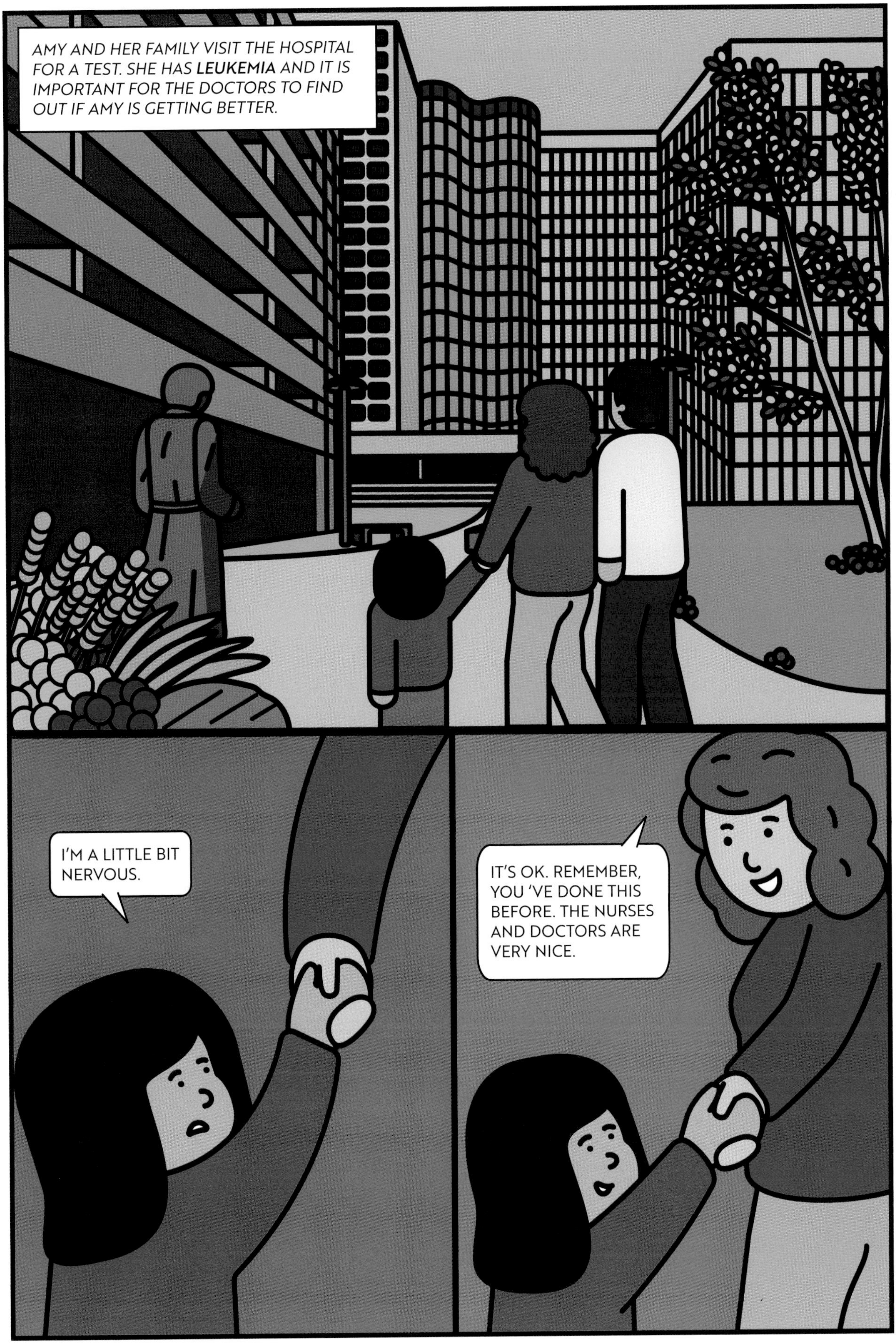
AMY AND HER FAMILY VISIT THE HOSPITAL FOR A TEST. SHE HAS **LEUKEMIA** AND IT IS IMPORTANT FOR THE DOCTORS TO FIND OUT IF AMY IS GETTING BETTER.
I'M A LITTLE BIT NERVOUS.
IT'S OK. REMEMBER, YOU 'VE DONE THIS BEFORE. THE NURSES AND DOCTORS ARE VERY NICE.

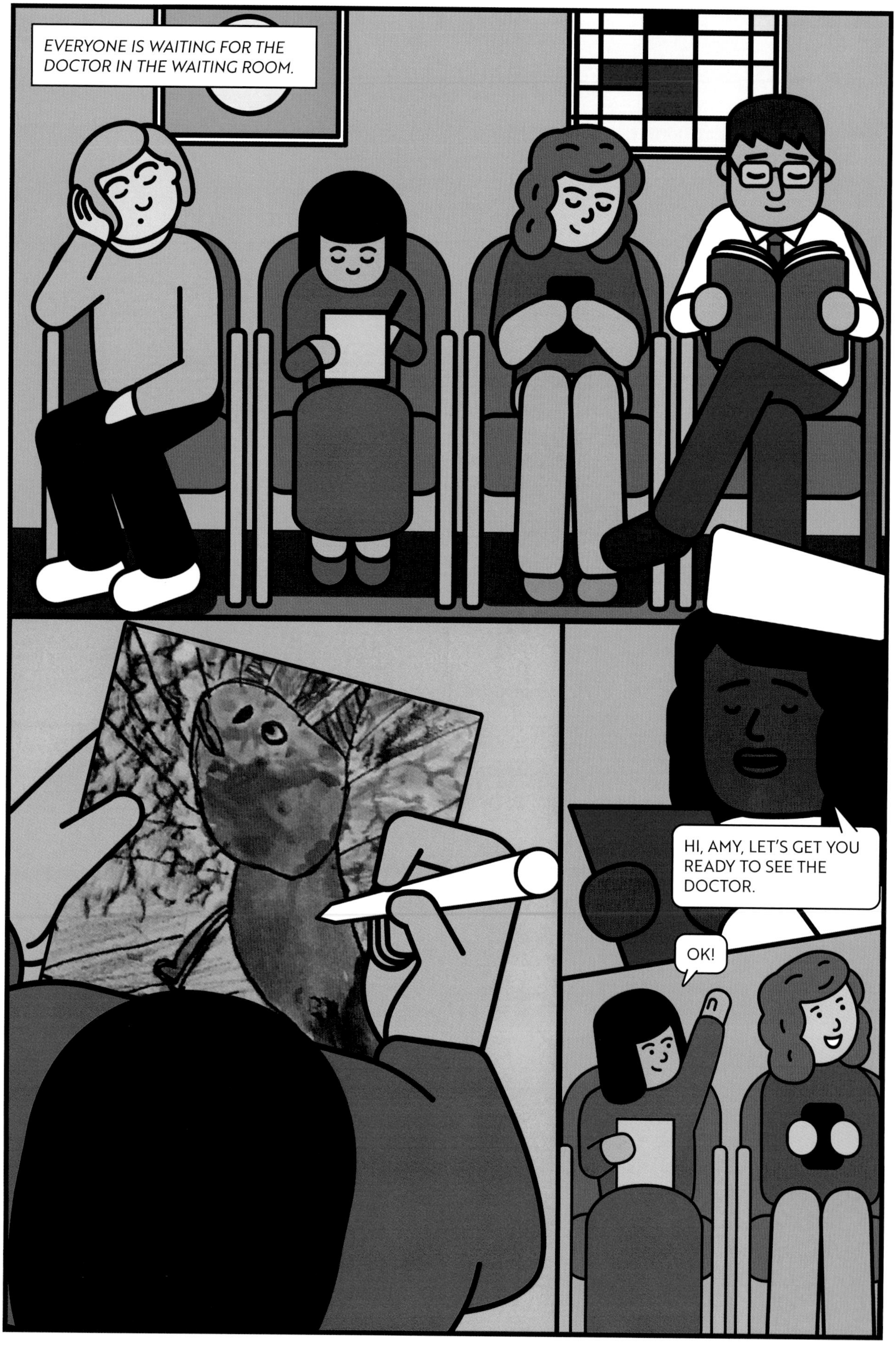
EVERYONE IS WAITING FOR THE DOCTOR IN THE WAITING ROOM.
HI, AMY, LET'S GET YOU READY TO SEE THE DOCTOR.
OK!

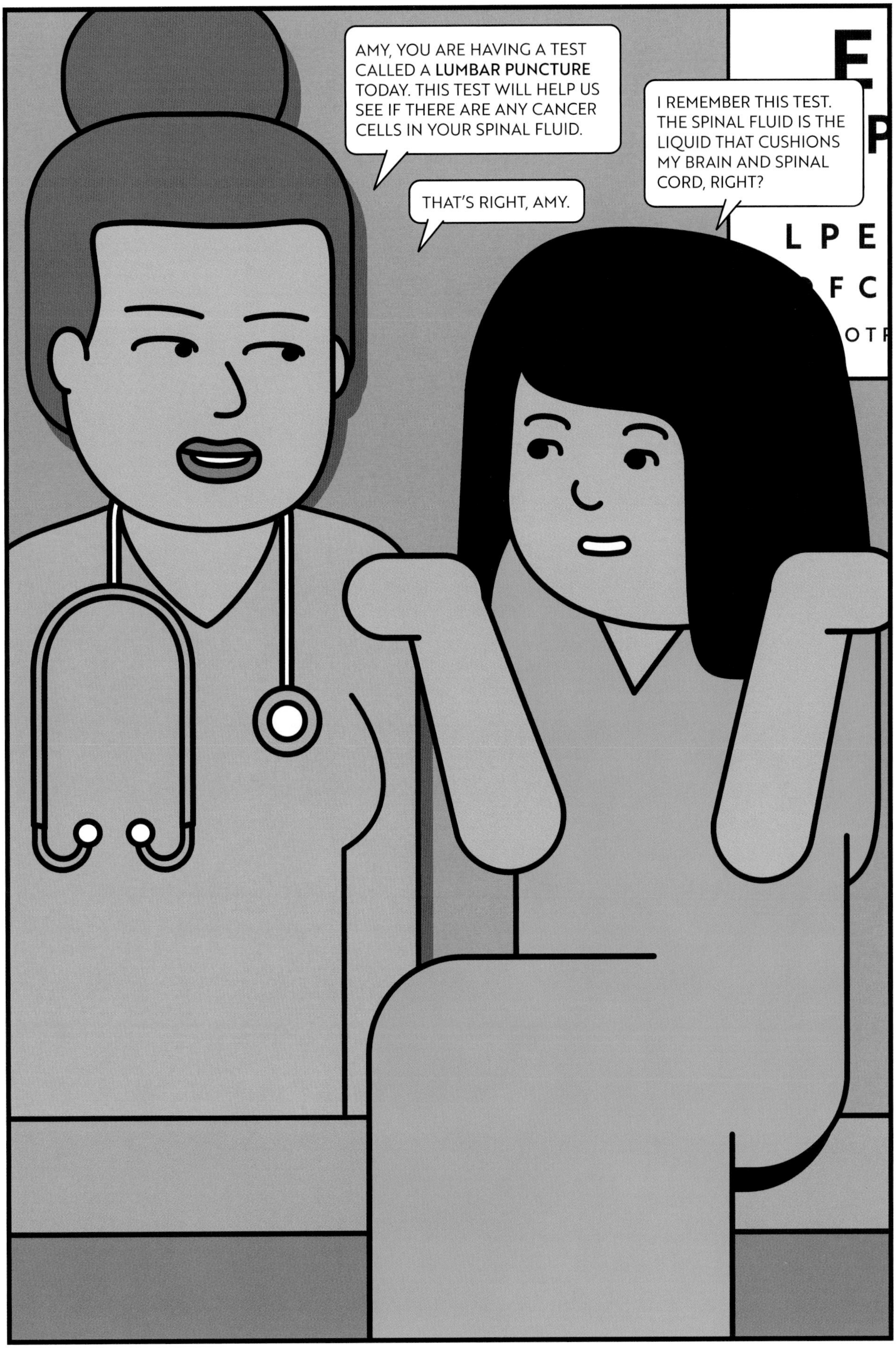
AMY, YOU ARE HAVING A TEST CALLED A **LUMBAR PUNCTURE** TODAY. THIS TEST WILL HELP US SEE IF THERE ARE ANY CANCER CELLS IN YOUR SPINAL FLUID.
THAT'S RIGHT, AMY.
I REMEMBER THIS TEST. THE SPINAL FLUID IS THE LIQUID THAT CUSHIONS MY BRAIN AND SPINAL CORD, RIGHT?
L P E
F C

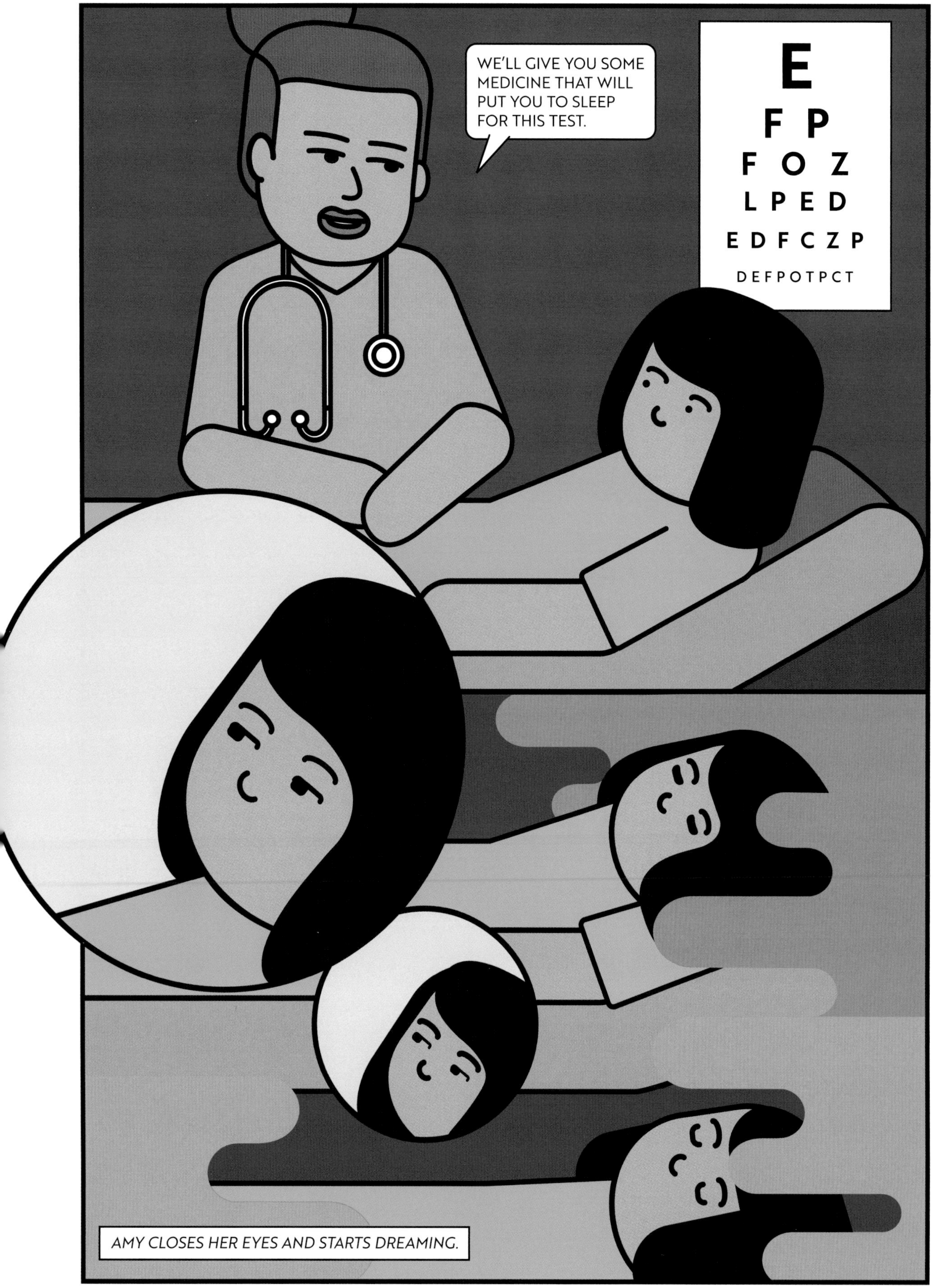
WE'LL GIVE YOU SOME MEDICINE THAT WILL PUT YOU TO SLEEP FOR THIS TEST.
E
F P
F O Z
L P E D
E D F C Z P
D E F P O T P C T
AMY CLOSES HER EYES AND STARTS DREAMING.

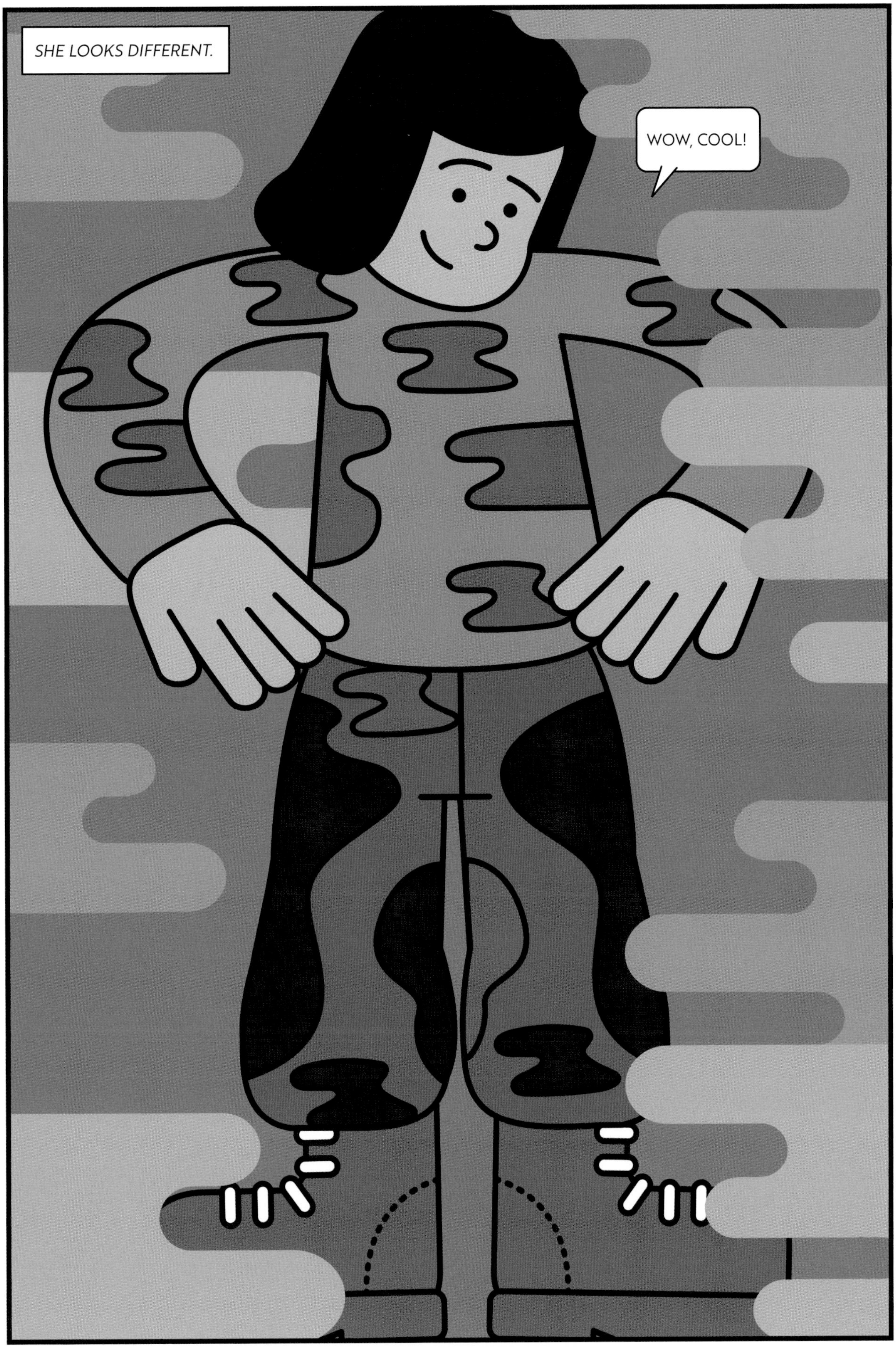
SHE LOOKS DIFFERENT.
WOW, COOL!

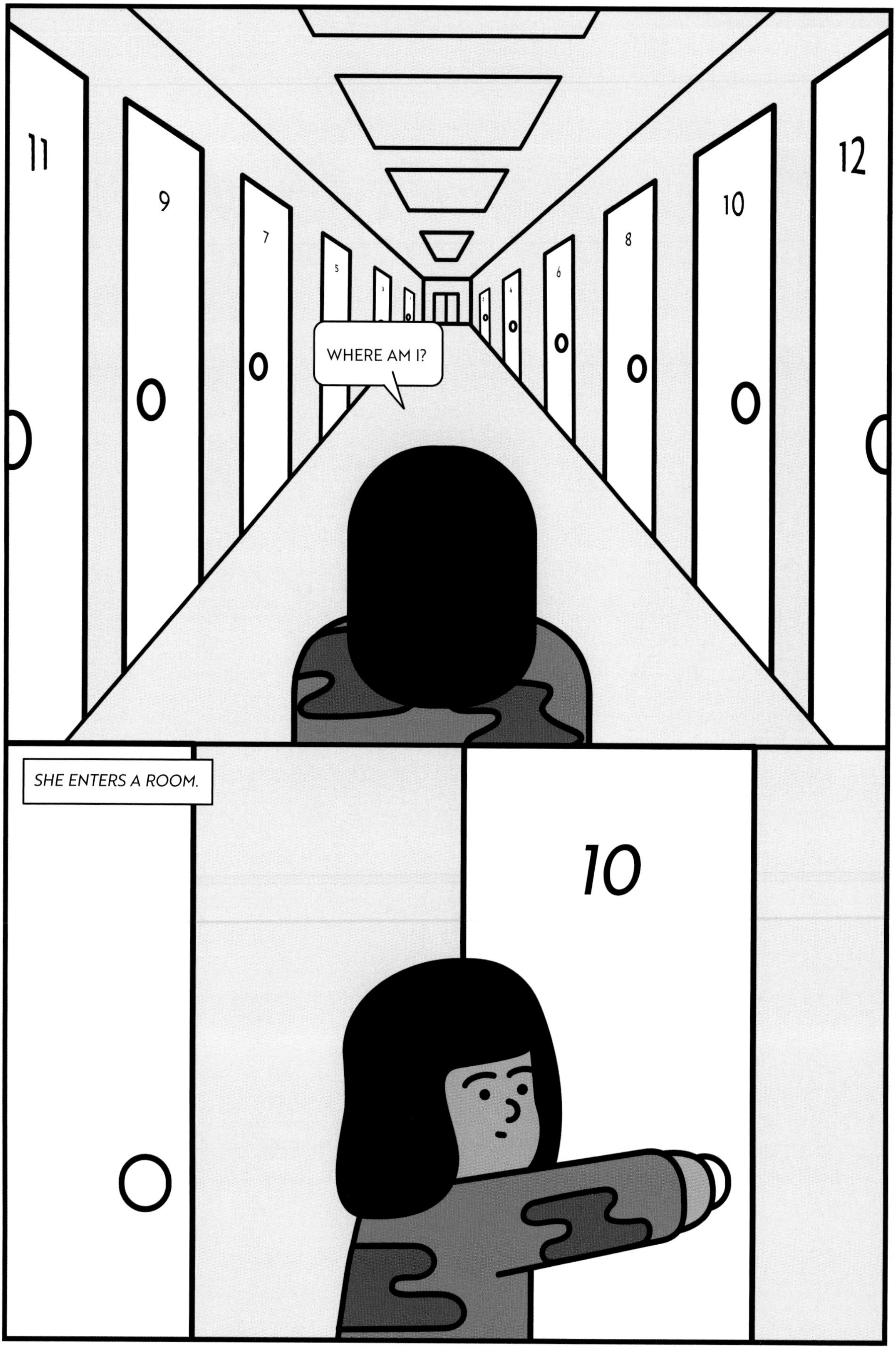
WHERE AM I?
SHE ENTERS A ROOM.
10

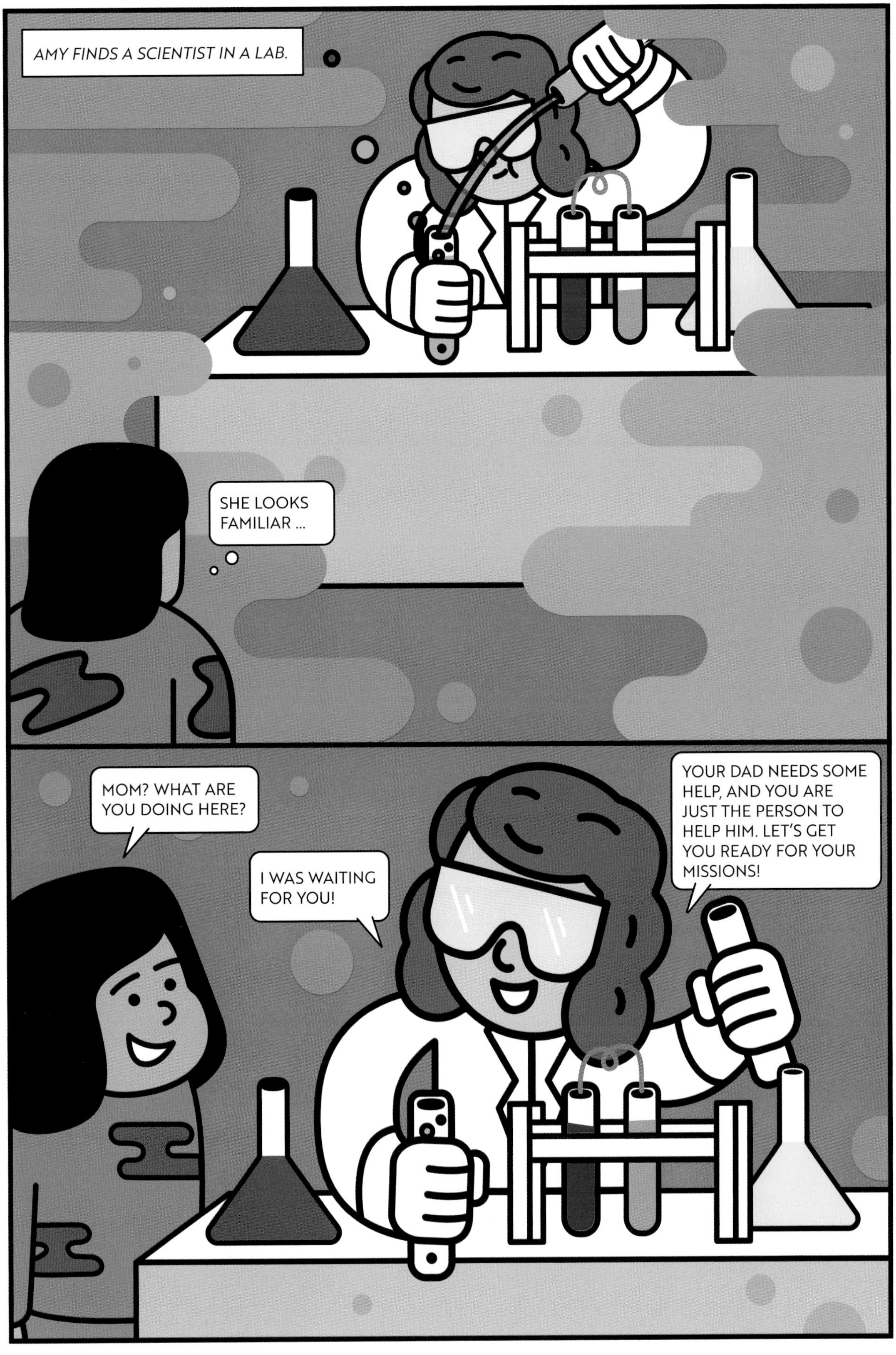

AMY FINDS A SCIENTIST IN A LAB.
SHE LOOKS FAMILIAR ...
MOM? WHAT ARE YOU DOING HERE?
I WAS WAITING FOR YOU!
YOUR DAD NEEDS SOME HELP, AND YOU ARE JUST THE PERSON TO HELP HIM. LET'S GET YOU READY FOR YOUR MISSIONS!

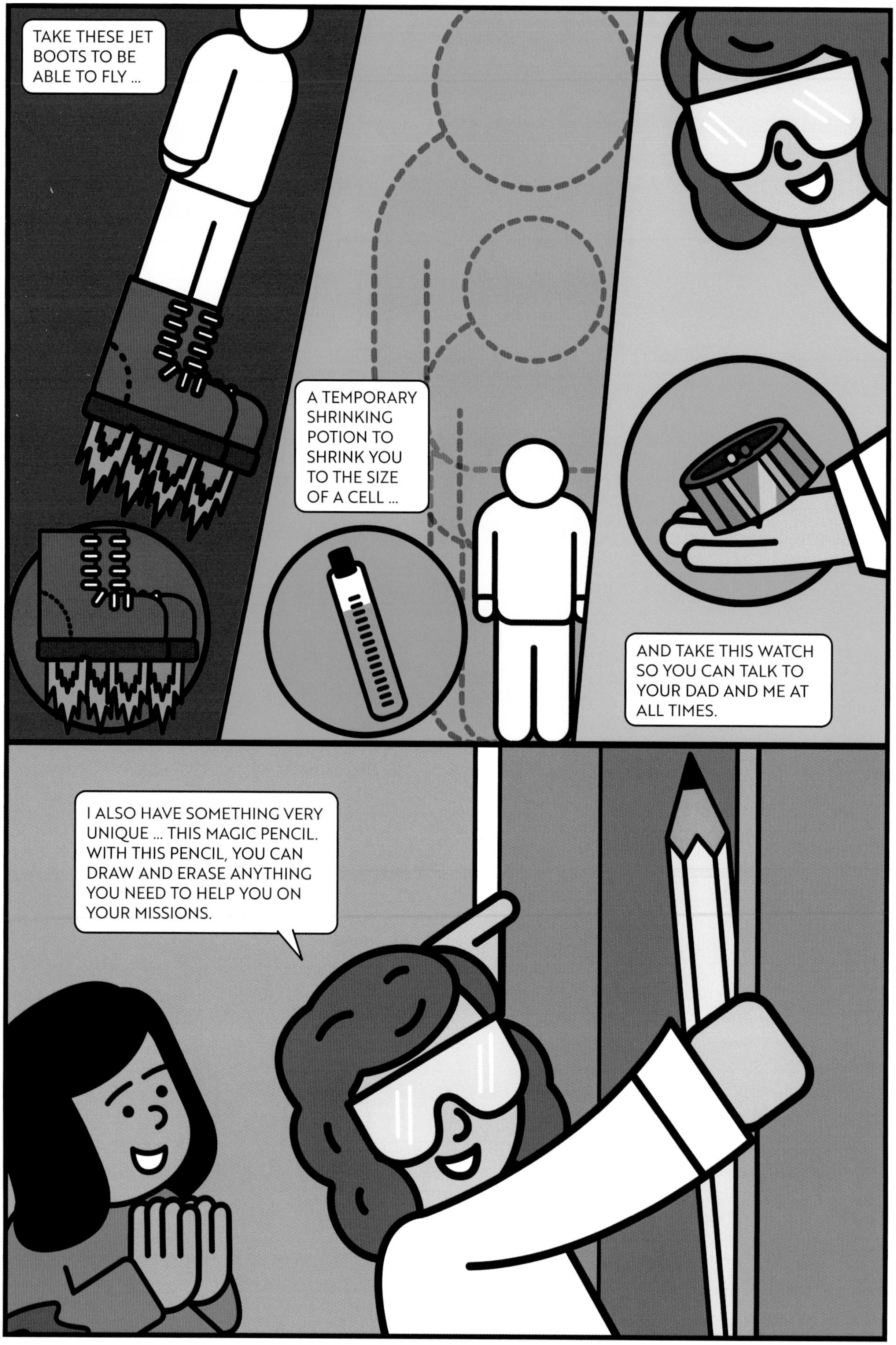
TAKE THESE JET BOOTS TO BE ABLE TO FLY ...
A TEMPORARY SHRINKING POTION TO SHRINK YOU TO THE SIZE OF A CELL ...
AND TAKE THIS WATCH SO YOU CAN TALK TO YOUR DAD AND ME AT ALL TIMES.
I ALSO HAVE SOMETHING VERY UNIQUE ... THIS MAGIC PENCIL. WITH THIS PENCIL, YOU CAN DRAW AND ERASE ANYTHING YOU NEED TO HELP YOU ON YOUR MISSIONS.

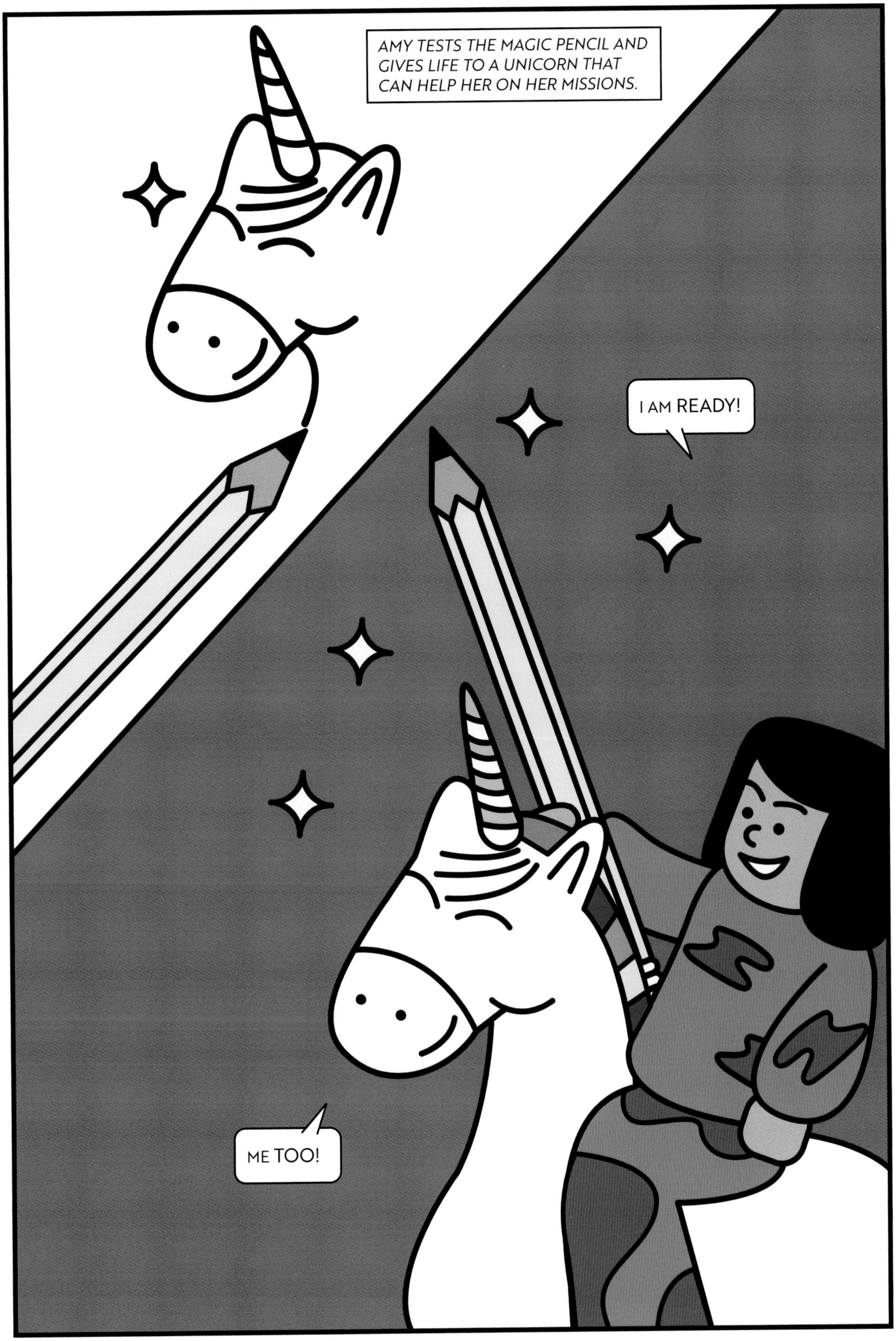
AMY TESTS THE MAGIC PENCIL AND GIVES LIFE TO A UNICORN THAT CAN HELP HER ON HER MISSIONS.
I AM READY!
ME TOO!

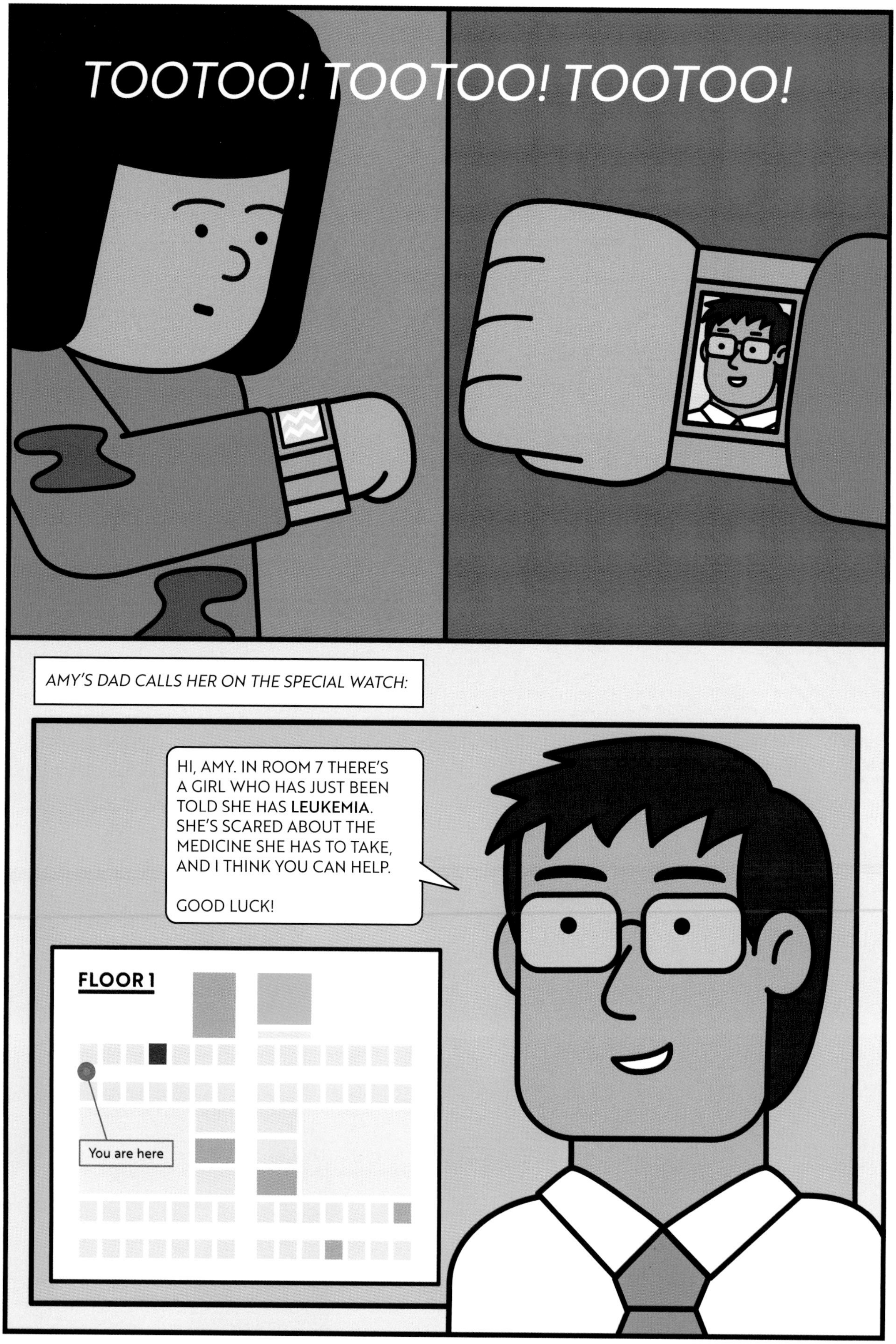
TOOTOO! TOOTOO! TOOTOO!
AMY'S DAD CALLS HER ON THE SPECIAL WATCH:
HI, AMY. IN ROOM 7 THERE'S A GIRL WHO HAS JUST BEEN TOLD SHE HAS **LEUKEMIA**. SHE'S SCARED ABOUT THE MEDICINE SHE HAS TO TAKE, AND I THINK YOU CAN HELP.
GOOD LUCK!
FLOOR 1
You are here

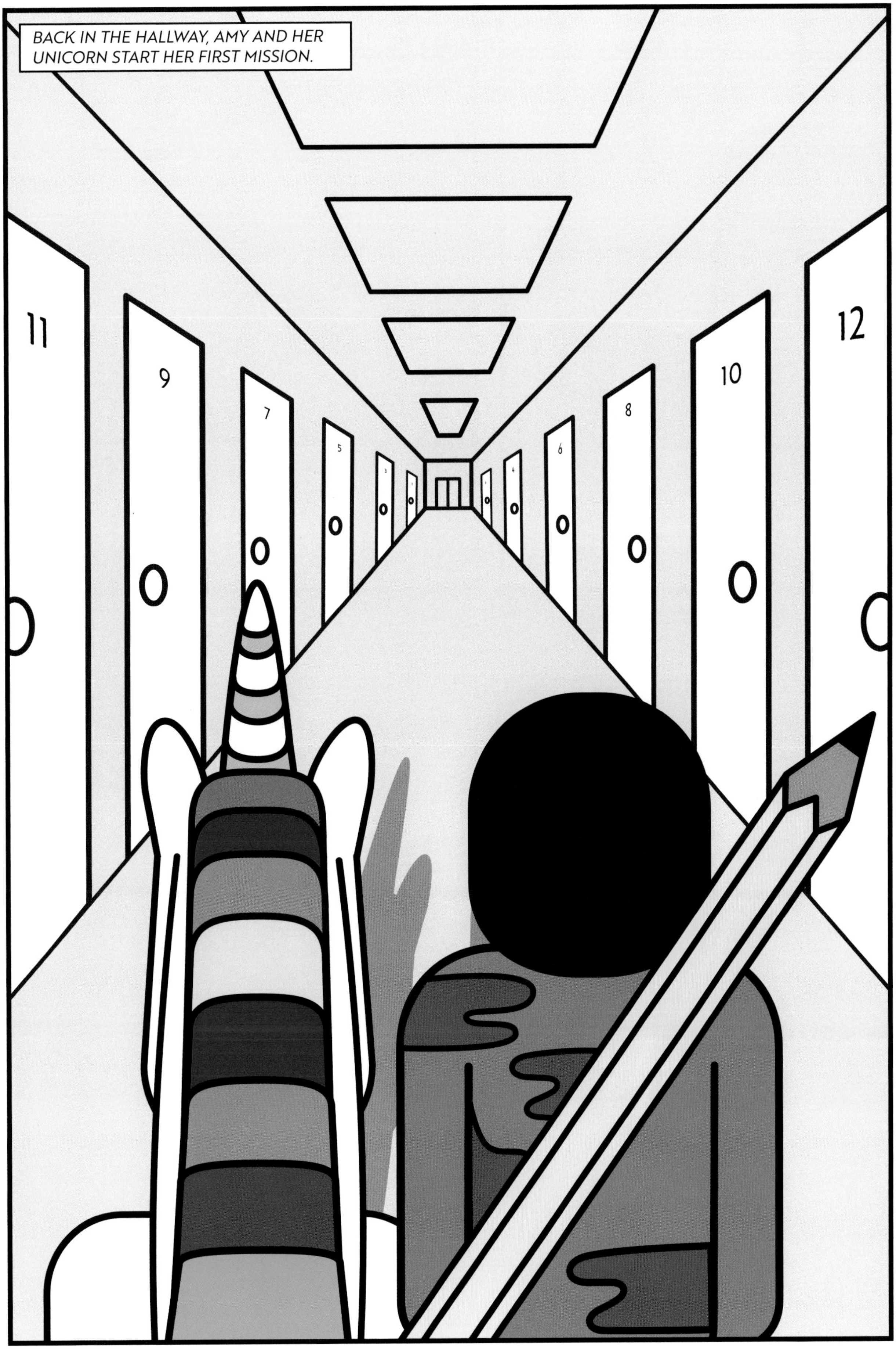
BACK IN THE HALLWAY, AMY AND HER UNICORN START HER FIRST MISSION.
11
9
7
5
12
10
8
6

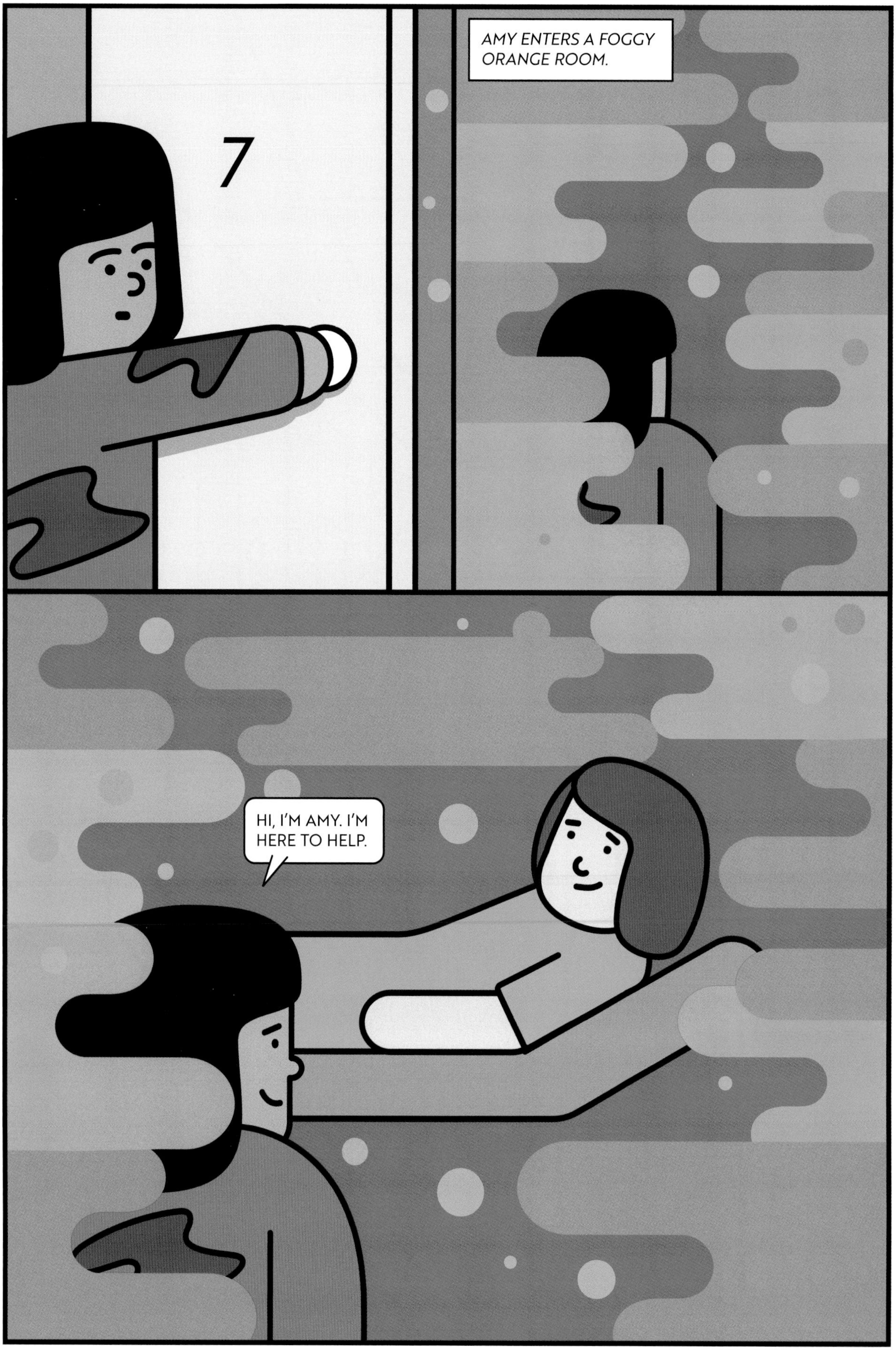
7
AMY ENTERS A FOGGY ORANGE ROOM.
HI, I'M AMY. I'M HERE TO HELP.

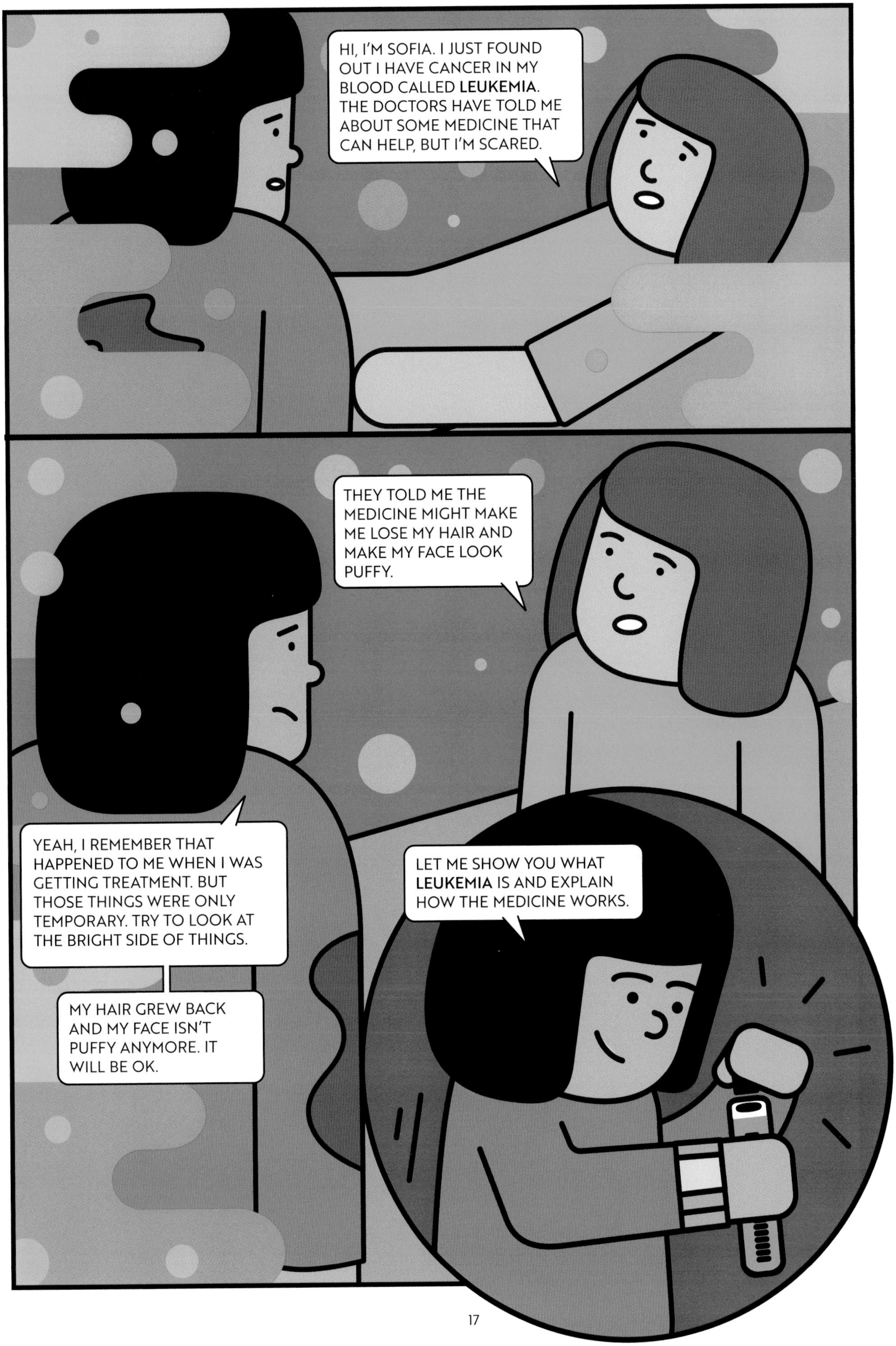
HI, I'M SOFIA. I JUST FOUND OUT I HAVE CANCER IN MY BLOOD CALLED **LEUKEMIA**. THE DOCTORS HAVE TOLD ME ABOUT SOME MEDICINE THAT CAN HELP, BUT I'M SCARED.
THEY TOLD ME THE MEDICINE MIGHT MAKE ME LOSE MY HAIR AND MAKE MY FACE LOOK PUFFY.
YEAH, I REMEMBER THAT HAPPENED TO ME WHEN I WAS GETTING TREATMENT. BUT THOSE THINGS WERE ONLY TEMPORARY. TRY TO LOOK AT THE BRIGHT SIDE OF THINGS.
MY HAIR GREW BACK AND MY FACE ISN'T PUFFY ANYMORE. IT WILL BE OK.
LET ME SHOW YOU WHAT **LEUKEMIA** IS AND EXPLAIN HOW THE MEDICINE WORKS.

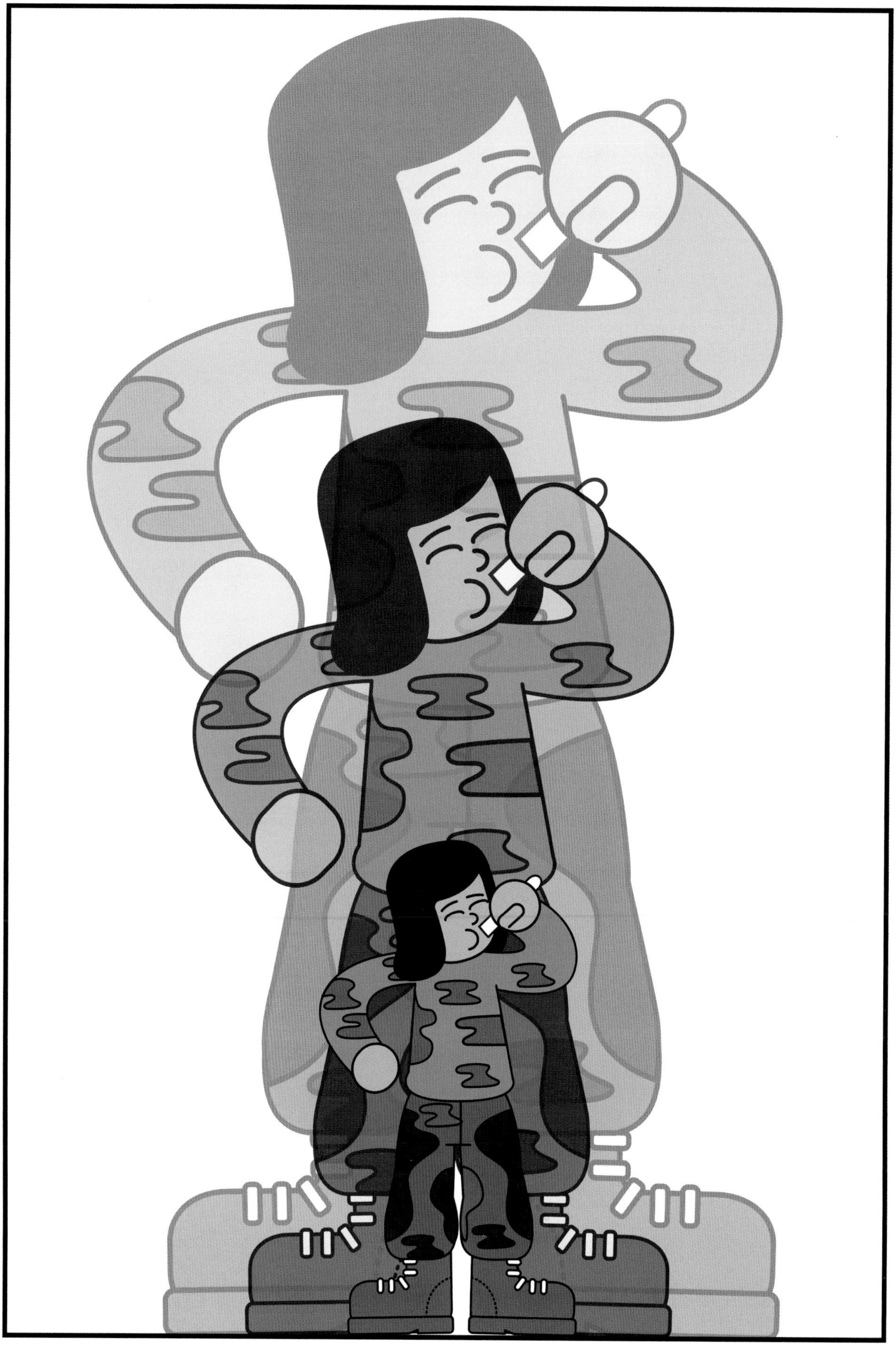

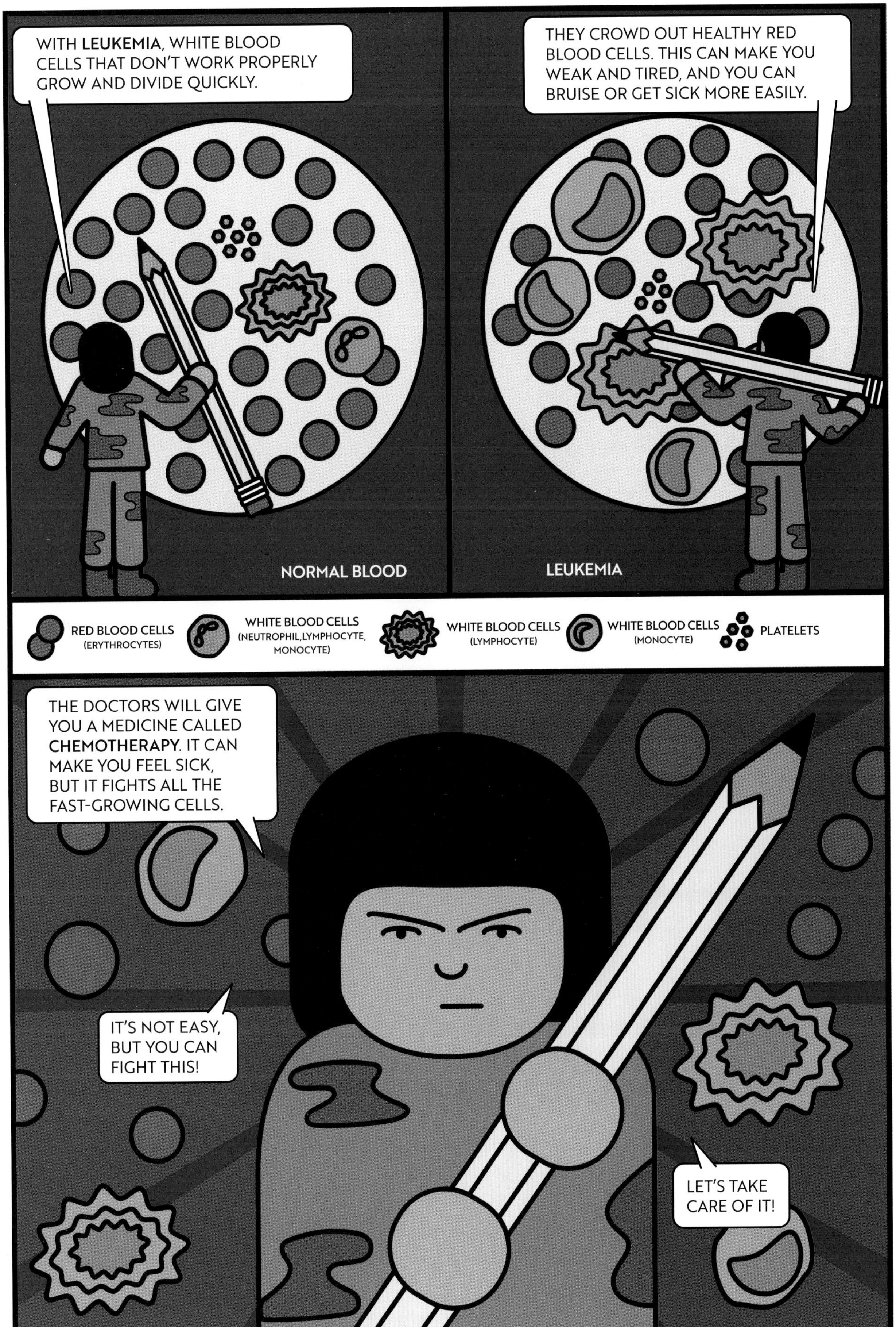
WITH LEUKEMIA, WHITE BLOOD CELLS THAT DON'T WORK PROPERLY GROW AND DIVIDE QUICKLY.
NORMAL BLOOD
THEY CROWD OUT HEALTHY RED BLOOD CELLS. THIS CAN MAKE YOU WEAK AND TIRED, AND YOU CAN BRUISE OR GET SICK MORE EASILY.
LEUKEMIA
RED BLOOD CELLS (ERYTHROCYTES)
WHITE BLOOD CELLS (NEUTROPHIL, LYMPHOCYTE, MONOCYTE)
WHITE BLOOD CELLS (LYMPHOCYTE)
WHITE BLOOD CELLS (MONOCYTE)
PLATELETS
THE DOCTORS WILL GIVE YOU A MEDICINE CALLED CHEMOTHERAPY. IT CAN MAKE YOU FEEL SICK, BUT IT FIGHTS ALL THE FAST-GROWING CELLS.
IT'S NOT EASY, BUT YOU CAN FIGHT THIS!
LET'S TAKE CARE OF IT!

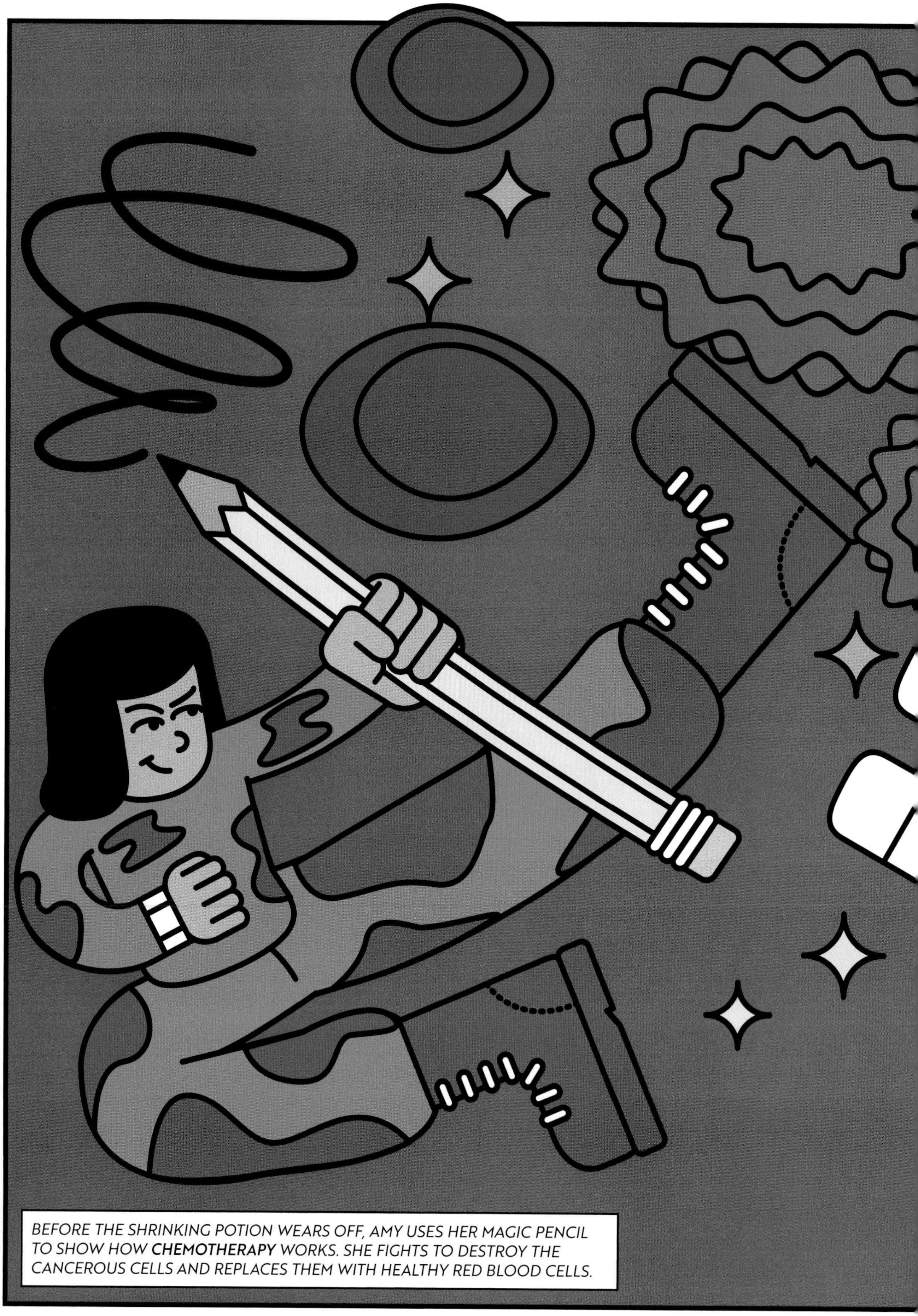
BEFORE THE SHRINKING POTION WEARS OFF, AMY USES HER MAGIC PENCIL TO SHOW HOW ***CHEMOTHERAPY*** *WORKS. SHE FIGHTS TO DESTROY THE CANCEROUS CELLS AND REPLACES THEM WITH HEALTHY RED BLOOD CELLS.*

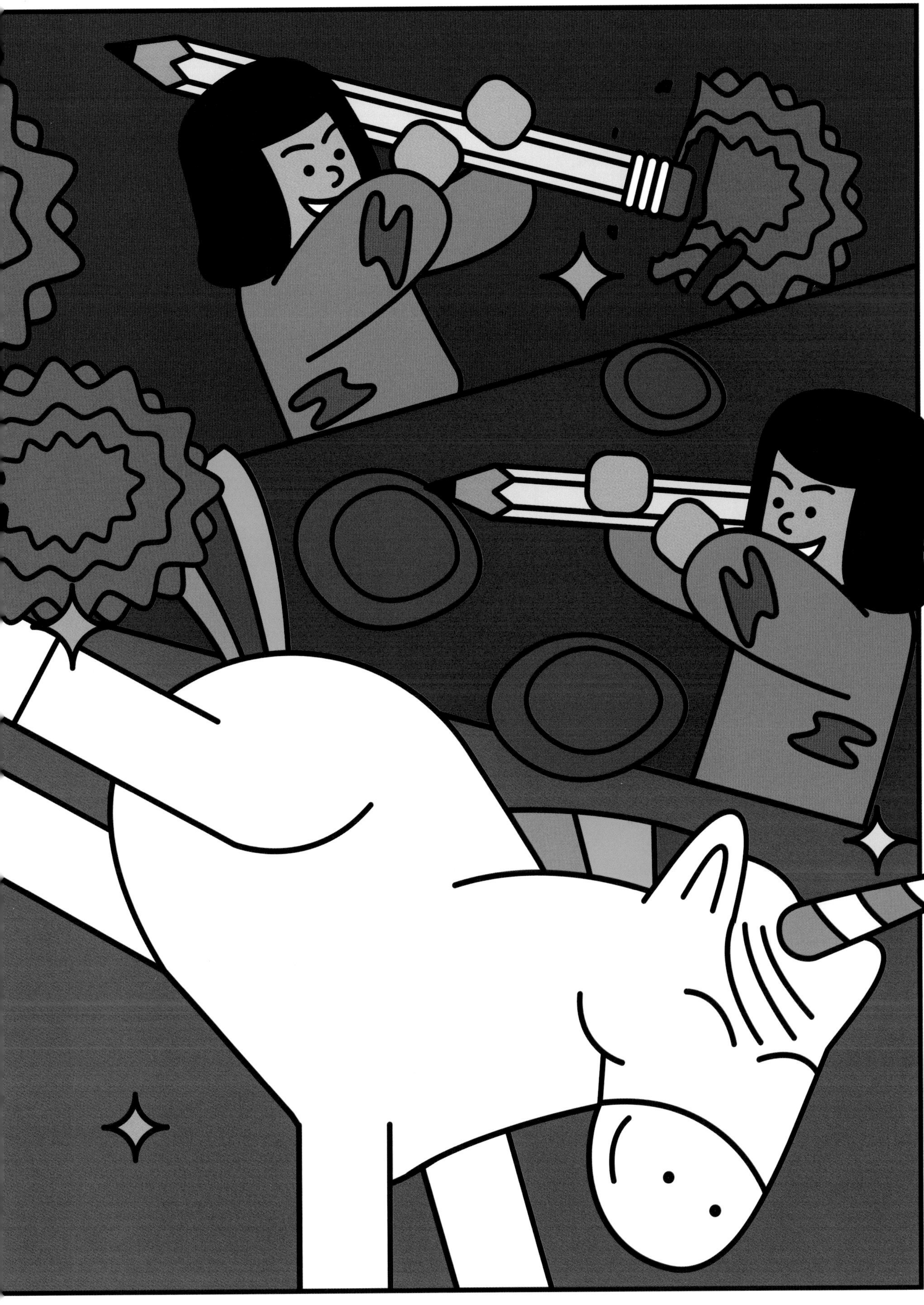

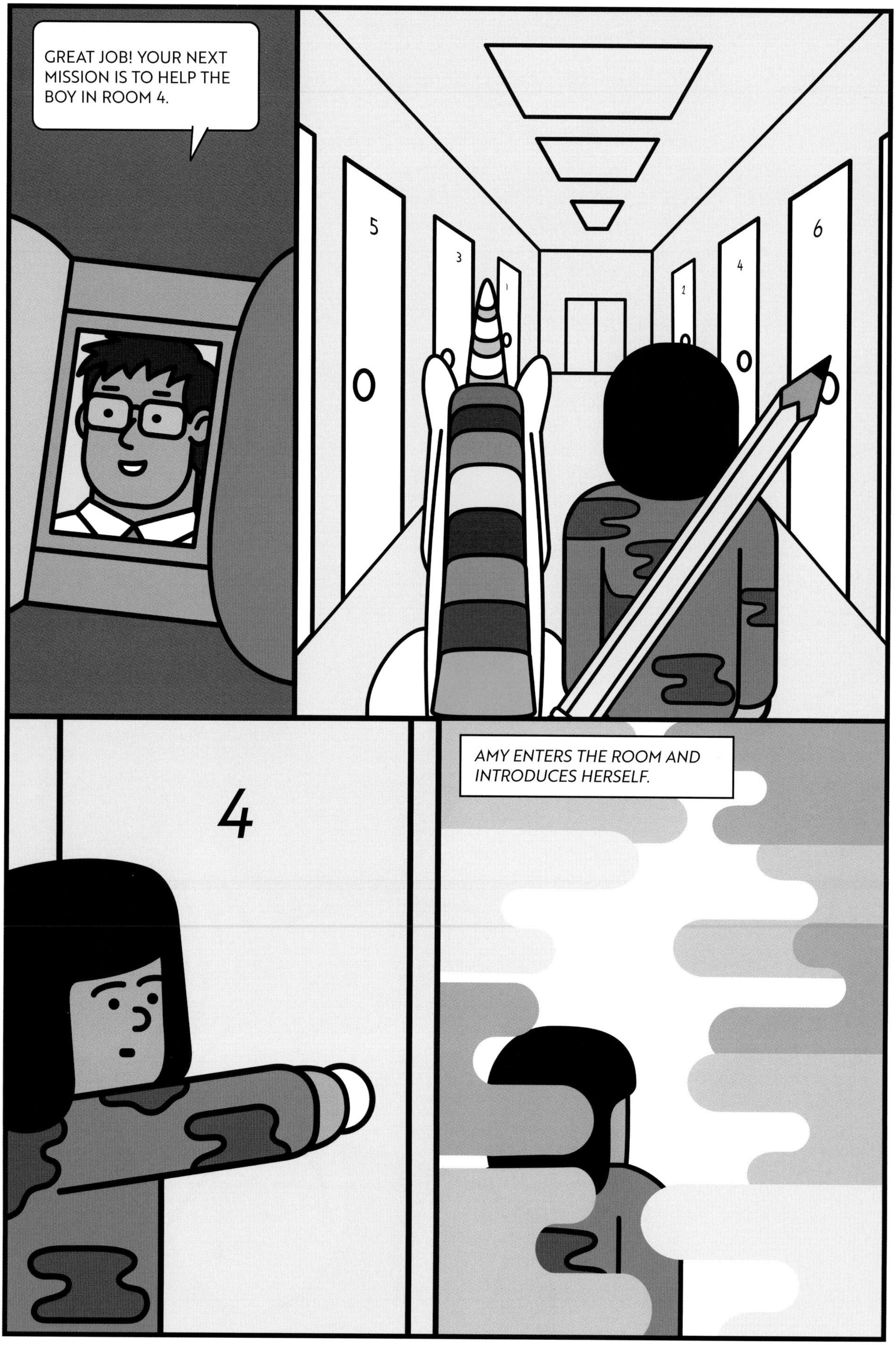
GREAT JOB! YOUR NEXT MISSION IS TO HELP THE BOY IN ROOM 4.
5
3
1
2
4
6
4
AMY ENTERS THE ROOM AND INTRODUCES HERSELF.

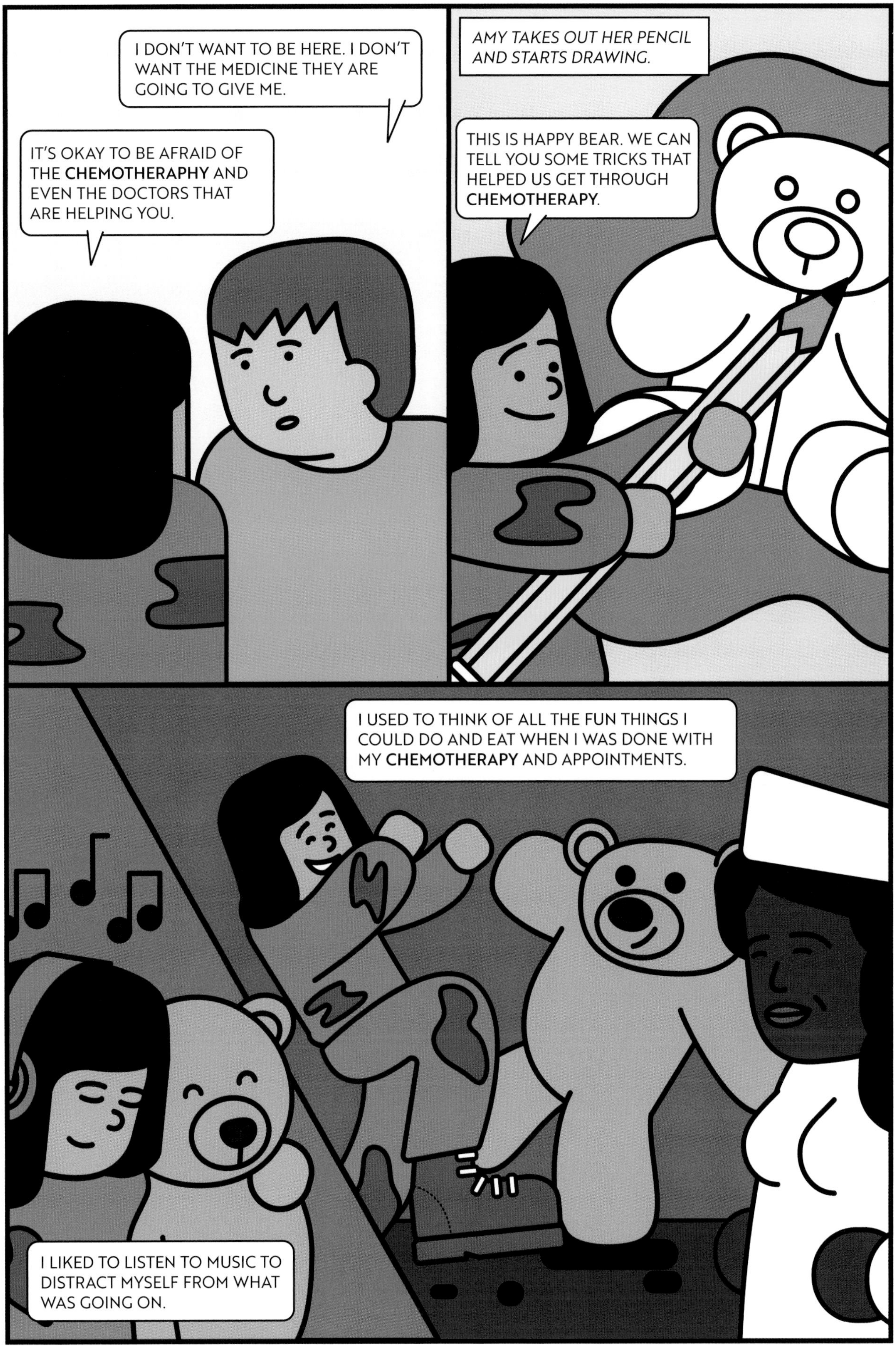
I DON'T WANT TO BE HERE. I DON'T WANT THE MEDICINE THEY ARE GOING TO GIVE ME.
IT'S OKAY TO BE AFRAID OF THE **CHEMOTHERAPHY** AND EVEN THE DOCTORS THAT ARE HELPING YOU.
AMY TAKES OUT HER PENCIL AND STARTS DRAWING.
THIS IS HAPPY BEAR. WE CAN TELL YOU SOME TRICKS THAT HELPED US GET THROUGH **CHEMOTHERAPY**.
I USED TO THINK OF ALL THE FUN THINGS I COULD DO AND EAT WHEN I WAS DONE WITH MY **CHEMOTHERAPY** AND APPOINTMENTS.
I LIKED TO LISTEN TO MUSIC TO DISTRACT MYSELF FROM WHAT WAS GOING ON.

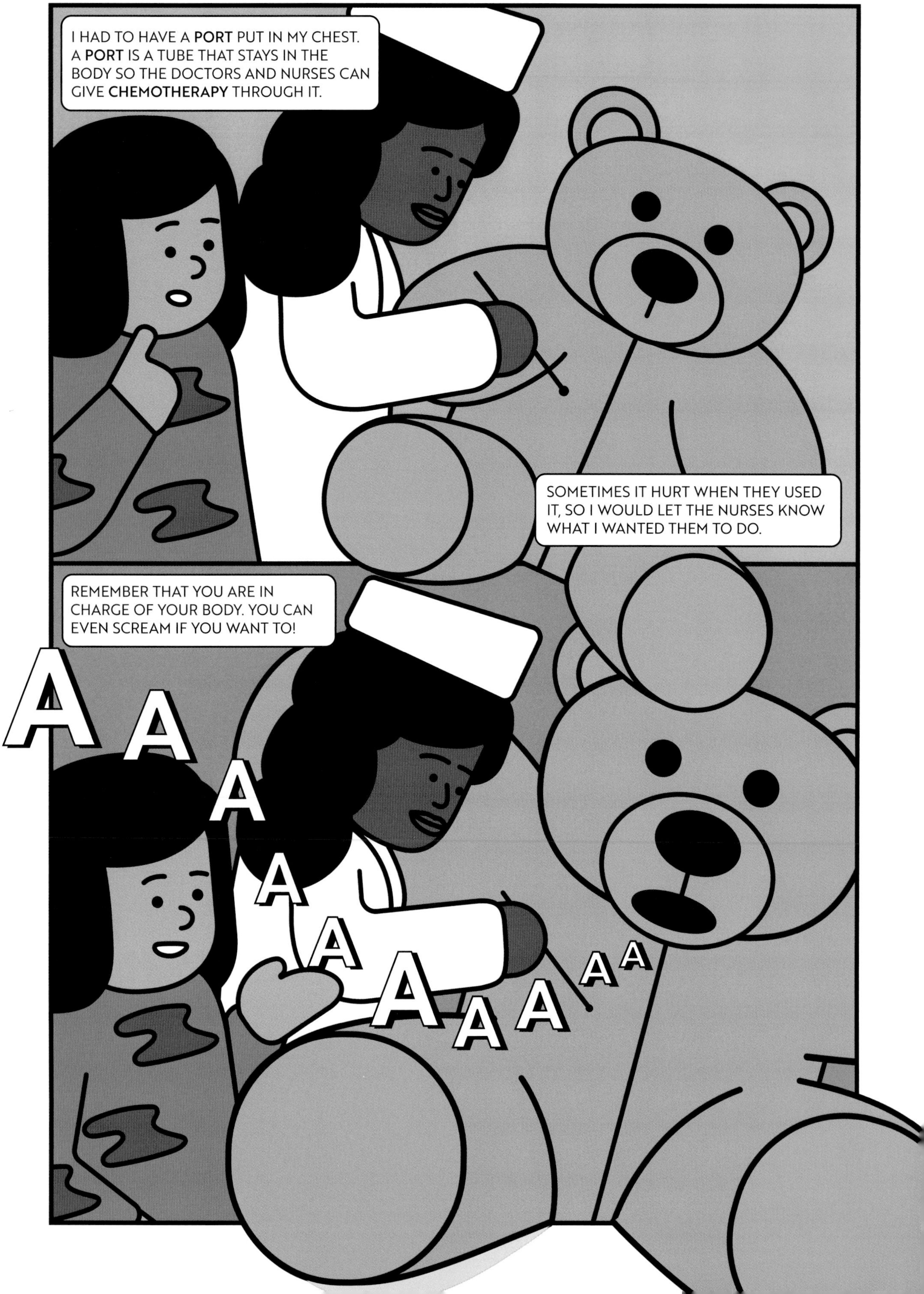
I HAD TO HAVE A **PORT** PUT IN MY CHEST. A **PORT** IS A TUBE THAT STAYS IN THE BODY SO THE DOCTORS AND NURSES CAN GIVE **CHEMOTHERAPY** THROUGH IT.
SOMETIMES IT HURT WHEN THEY USED IT, SO I WOULD LET THE NURSES KNOW WHAT I WANTED THEM TO DO.
REMEMBER THAT YOU ARE IN CHARGE OF YOUR BODY. YOU CAN EVEN SCREAM IF YOU WANT TO!
AAAAAAAAAAA

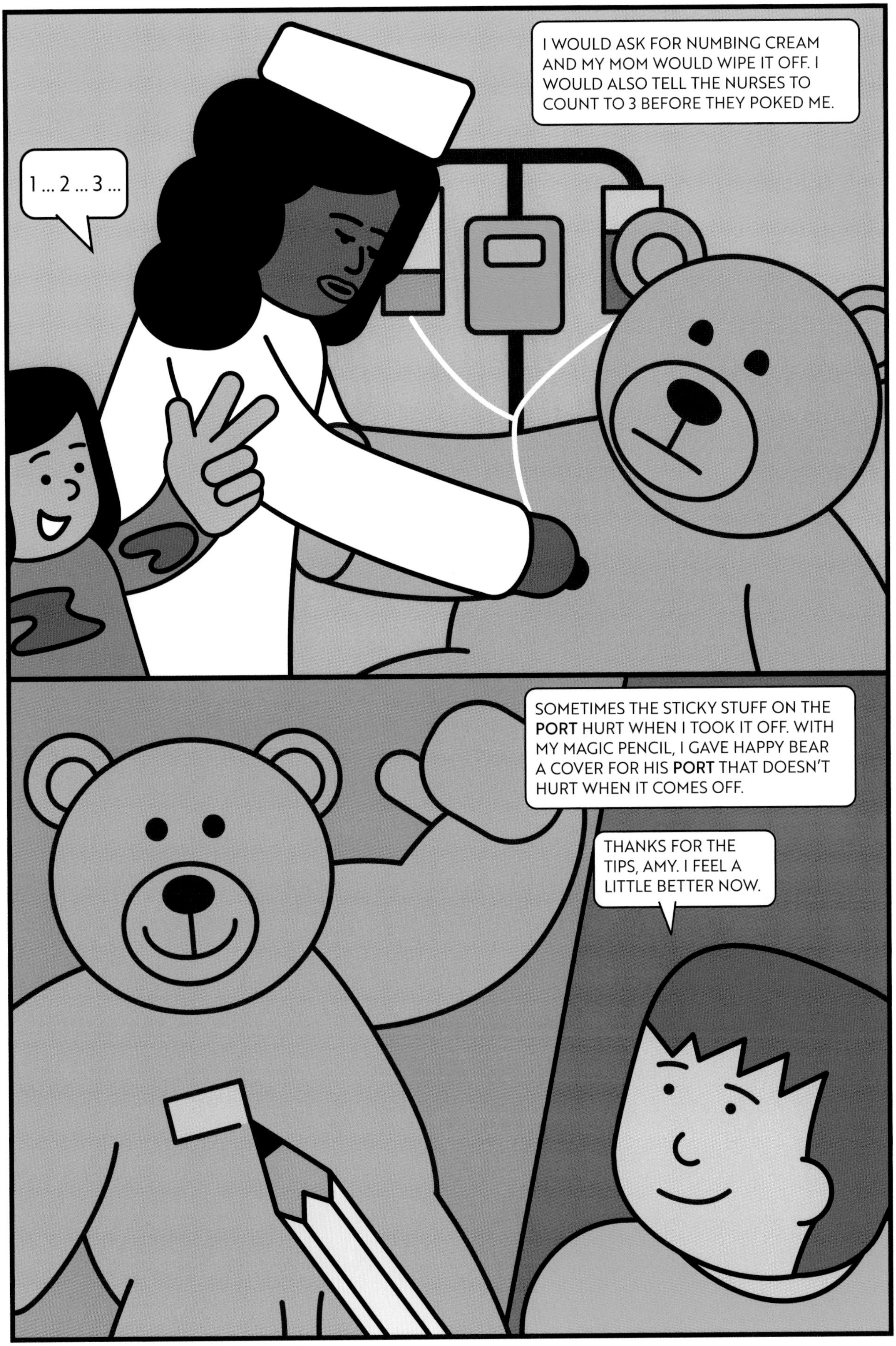
I WOULD ASK FOR NUMBING CREAM AND MY MOM WOULD WIPE IT OFF. I WOULD ALSO TELL THE NURSES TO COUNT TO 3 BEFORE THEY POKED ME.
1 ... 2 ... 3 ...
SOMETIMES THE STICKY STUFF ON THE **PORT** HURT WHEN I TOOK IT OFF. WITH MY MAGIC PENCIL, I GAVE HAPPY BEAR A COVER FOR HIS **PORT** THAT DOESN'T HURT WHEN IT COMES OFF.
THANKS FOR THE TIPS, AMY. I FEEL A LITTLE BETTER NOW.

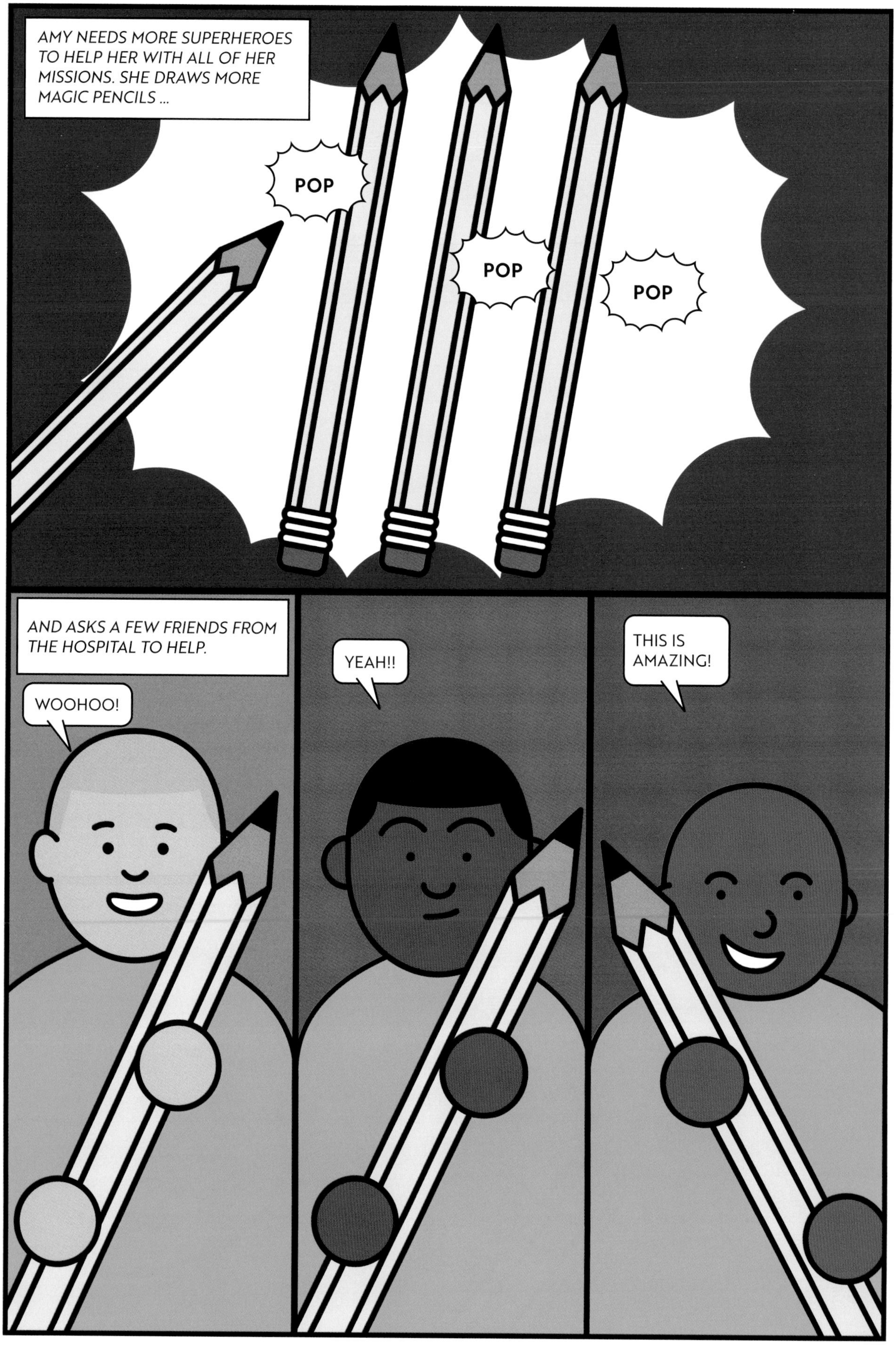
AMY NEEDS MORE SUPERHEROES TO HELP HER WITH ALL OF HER MISSIONS. SHE DRAWS MORE MAGIC PENCILS ...
POP
POP
POP
AND ASKS A FEW FRIENDS FROM THE HOSPITAL TO HELP.
WOOHOO!
YEAH!!
THIS IS AMAZING!

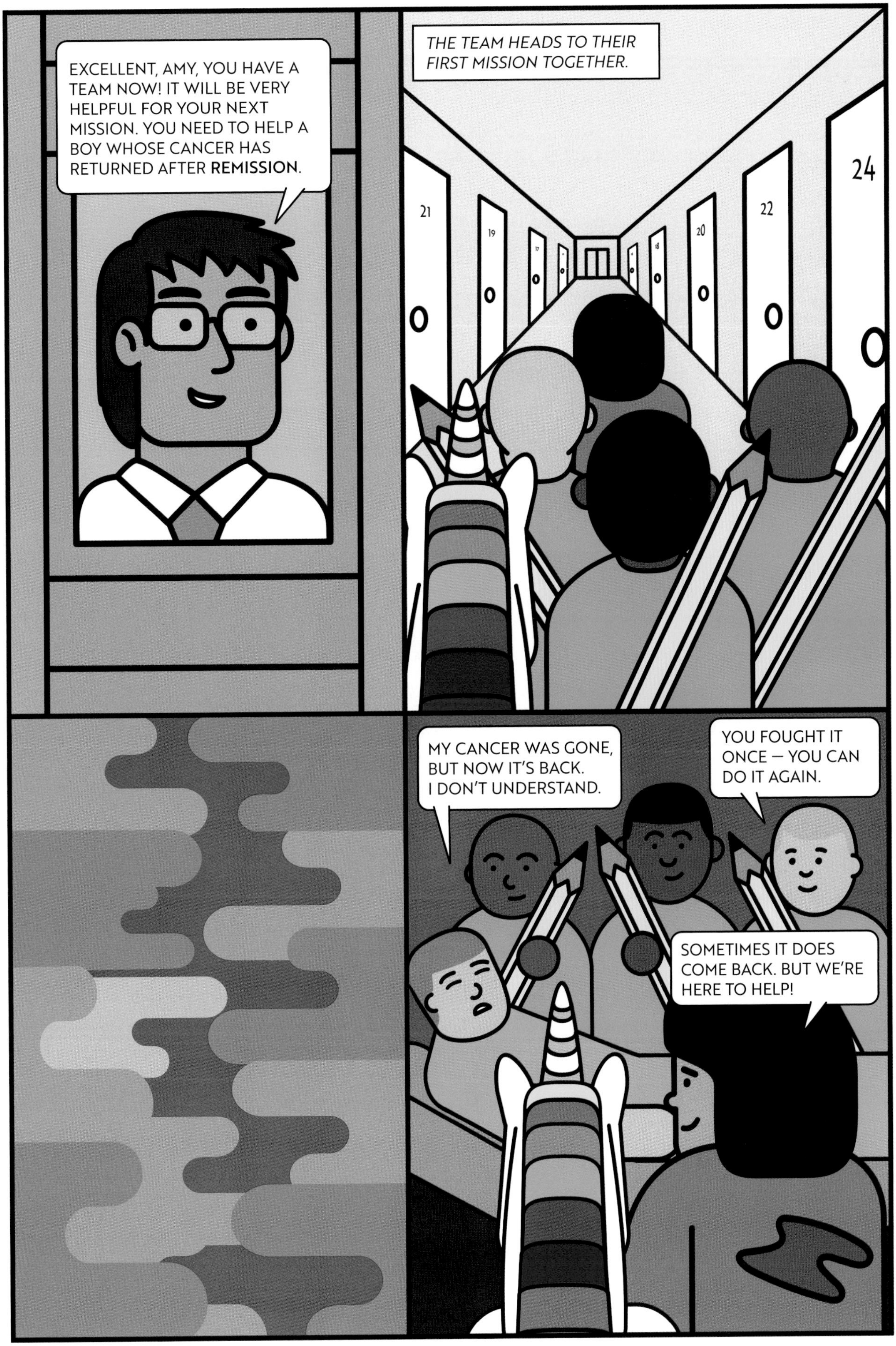
EXCELLENT, AMY, YOU HAVE A TEAM NOW! IT WILL BE VERY HELPFUL FOR YOUR NEXT MISSION. YOU NEED TO HELP A BOY WHOSE CANCER HAS RETURNED AFTER **REMISSION**.
THE TEAM HEADS TO THEIR FIRST MISSION TOGETHER.
24
22
21
20
19
MY CANCER WAS GONE, BUT NOW IT'S BACK. I DON'T UNDERSTAND.
YOU FOUGHT IT ONCE — YOU CAN DO IT AGAIN.
SOMETIMES IT DOES COME BACK. BUT WE'RE HERE TO HELP!

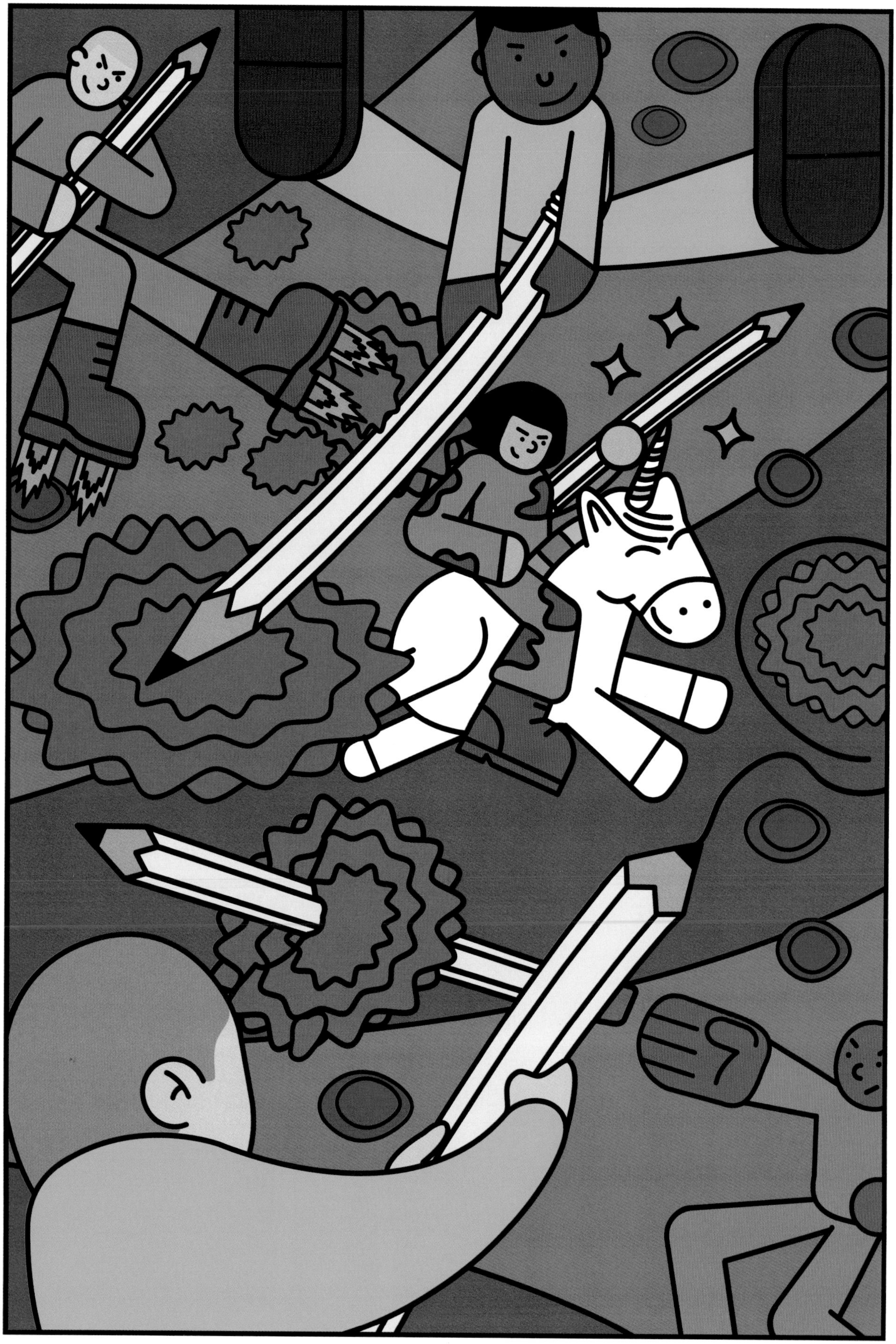

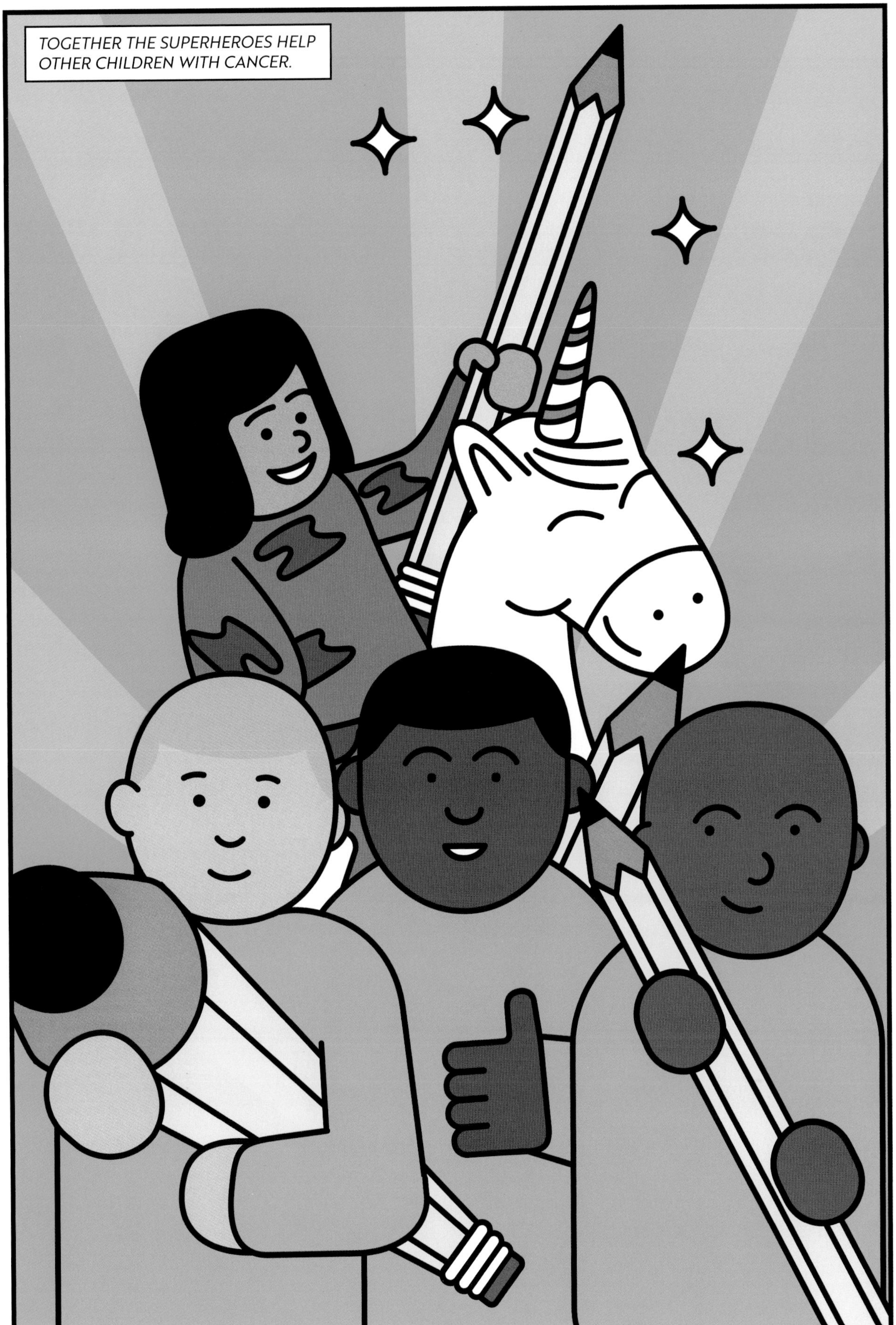
TOGETHER THE SUPERHEROES HELP OTHER CHILDREN WITH CANCER.

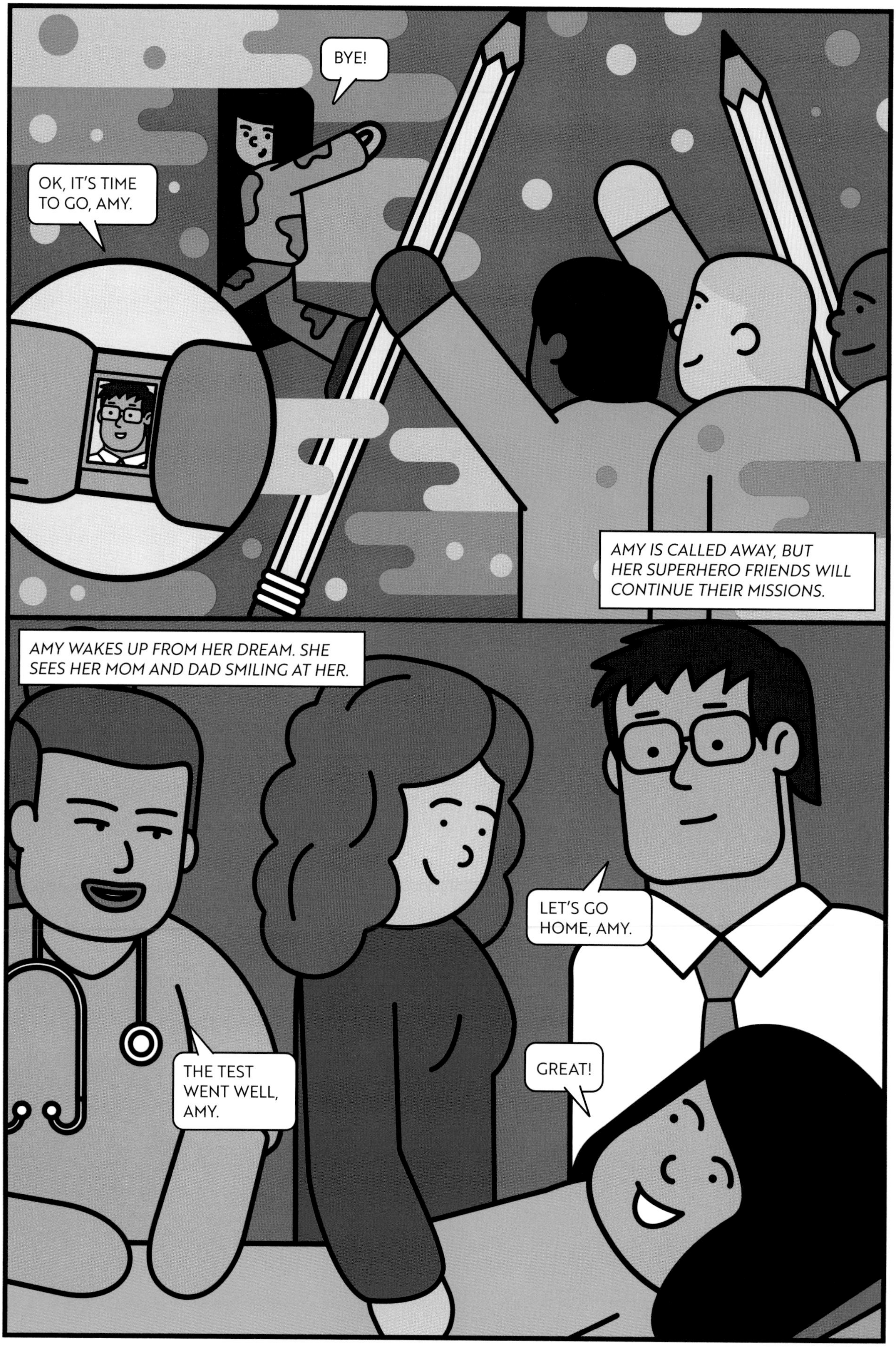
BYE!
OK, IT'S TIME TO GO, AMY.
AMY IS CALLED AWAY, BUT HER SUPERHERO FRIENDS WILL CONTINUE THEIR MISSIONS.
AMY WAKES UP FROM HER DREAM. SHE SEES HER MOM AND DAD SMILING AT HER.
LET'S GO HOME, AMY.
THE TEST WENT WELL, AMY.
GREAT!

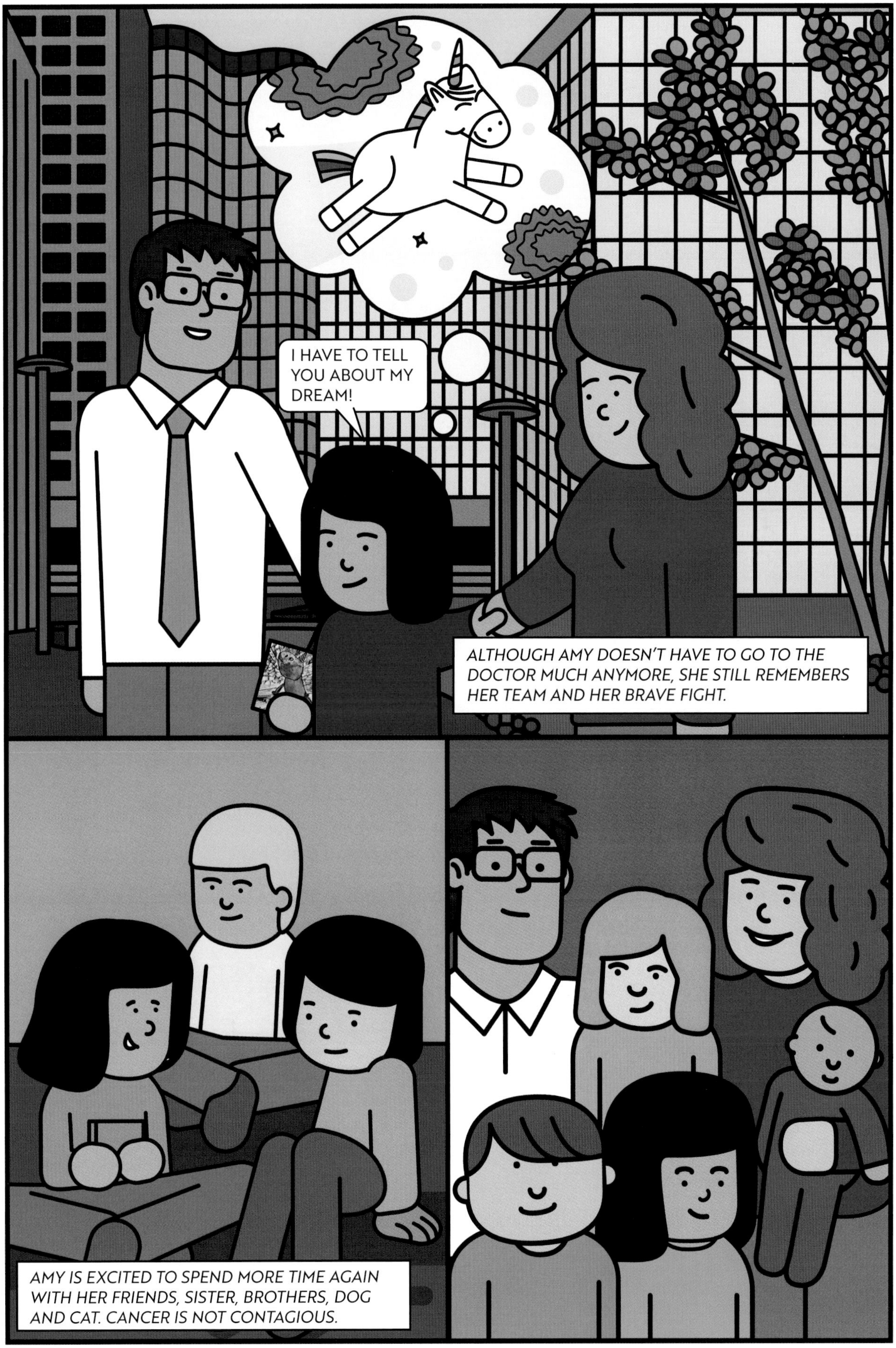
I HAVE TO TELL YOU ABOUT MY DREAM!
ALTHOUGH AMY DOESN'T HAVE TO GO TO THE DOCTOR MUCH ANYMORE, SHE STILL REMEMBERS HER TEAM AND HER BRAVE FIGHT.
AMY IS EXCITED TO SPEND MORE TIME AGAIN WITH HER FRIENDS, SISTER, BROTHERS, DOG AND CAT. CANCER IS NOT CONTAGIOUS.

KEY TERMS

ALL: acute lymphoblastic leukemia

AML: acute myeloid leukemia

bone marrow biopsy: a procedure to collect bone marrow cells from the back of the hip bone using a specific type of needle. This procedure is also typically done under anesthesia (medicine that puts the child to sleep). Bone marrow evaluation is needed for diagnosis and for monitoring treatment response.

chemotherapy: a strong medicine that kills cancer cells

immune system: system in the body that helps defend against infections, bacteria and viruses

lumbar puncture: a procedure used to collect spinal fluid from the back. This can be used to look for leukemia cells and also to give chemotherapy to the spinal fluid to prevent leukemia from growing there. Children typically get special medicine to help them fall asleep for this procedure.

port: a special intravenous (IV) line that is placed by a surgeon underneath the skin and looks like a button. This provides safe and secure IV access to give medicine and to also get blood drawn for laboratory tests. The port can be easily accessed with a needle that is connected to tubing. Accessing the port can be painful, so numbing medicine is used ahead of time.

remission: when cancer is no longer detected in the body

MORE INFORMATION FROM THE MEDICAL EDITOR

By Mira A. Kohorst, M.D.
Consultant, Department of Pediatric Hematology and Oncology, Mayo Clinic,
Rochester, MN; Assistant Professor of Pediatric Hematology and Oncology,
Mayo Clinic College of Medicine and Science

Leukemia is a type of cancer affecting the blood and is the most common kind of childhood cancer. Blood is made up of different types of cells which are formed in the bone marrow, the body's blood factory. With leukemia, the bone marrow makes abnormal blood cells that multiply in an uncontrolled fashion. These rapidly expanding cells push out other normal cells and can cause bone pain, fevers, swollen lymph nodes, bleeding and bruising from low platelets and low energy from low red blood cells.

A diagnosis of leukemia is made based off a patient history, a physical examination, blood tests and a **bone marrow biopsy**. There are many different types of leukemia. Children usually have the fast growing type called acute leukemia. There are two main forms of acute leukemia in children: acute lymphoblastic leukemia (**ALL**) and acute myeloid leukemia (**AML**), with **ALL** being the more common of the two.

To treat leukemia, strong medicine called **chemotherapy** that kills cancer cells is needed. Children receive these medications by mouth, by vein (IV) and even directly into the spinal fluid in the back, since the leukemia can travel there. In some scenarios, radiation therapy may be needed to help treat leukemia. For leukemia that is not fully killed by standard **chemotherapy,** or for leukemia that goes away and comes back, a bone marrow transplant may be needed. Other new exciting therapies are always being developed and may be applied as well.

Children are considered in **remission** once their leukemia is no longer detectable in the bone marrow. Even after a child is considered to be in **remission**, a long treatment course is often needed to reduce the chance of the leukemia returning. For children with **ALL**, this course is typically 2-3 years with the most intense **chemotherapy** in the first few months. After treatment is complete, children require frequent check-ups to monitor for any signs of leukemia coming back and to watch for long-term side effects of the treatment. The cure rate for childhood leukemia has improved dramatically in the last several decades, with more and more survivors. These survivors are often left with health problems related to their intensive treatment. A multidisciplinary team typically follows these children into adulthood to help if any issues do arise.

REFERENCES

Kaplan JA. Leukemia in Children. *Pediatrics in Review*. 2019; doi: 10.1542/pir.2018-0192.

Brown P, Inaba H, Annesley C, Beck J, Colace S, Dallas M, DeSantes K, Kelly K, Kitko C, Lacayo N, Larrier N, Maese L, Mahadeo K, Nanda R, Nardi V, Rodriguez V, Rossoff J, Schuettpelz L, Silverman L, Sun J, Sun W, Teachey D, Wong V, Yanik G, Johnson-Chilla A, Ogba N. Pediatric Acute Lymphoblastic Leukemia, Version 2.2020, NCCN Clinical Practice Guidelines in Oncology. *Journal of the National Comprehensive Cancer Network*. 2020; doi: 10.6004/jnccn.2020.0001.

WEB RESOURCES

American Cancer Society — www.cancer.org
The American Cancer Society's mission is to free the world from cancer. Until they do, they'll be funding and conducting research, sharing expert information, supporting patients, and spreading the word about prevention.
All so you can live longer — and better.

Cure Search for Children's Cancer — www.curesearch.org
Cure Search for Children's Cancer is driving critical collaborations to accelerate the pace of pediatric drug development. They identify and fund innovative research with the potential to move quickly into the clinic and marketplace, reaching children now — not 10-20 years from now.

ABOUT THE MEDICAL EDITOR

Mira A. Kohorst, M.D.
Consultant, Department of Pediatric Hematology and Oncology, Mayo Clinic, Rochester, MN; Assistant Professor of Pediatric Hematology and Oncology, Mayo Clinic College of Medicine and Science
Dr. Kohorst is board certified in Pediatric Hematology Oncology and Clinical Pharmacology. She is an Assistant Professor of Pediatric Hematology Oncology at Mayo Clinic College of Medicine and Science in Rochester, MN. Dr. Kohorst has published 16 peer-reviewed articles, book chapters and numerous abstracts for national and international meetings. Her focus is pediatric hematopoietic cell transplantation, cellular therapy and high risk leukemia and lymphoma.

ABOUT THE AUTHORS

Guillaume Federighi, aka **Hey Gee**, is a French and American author and illustrator. He began his career in 1998 in Paris, France. He also spent a few decades exploring the world of street art and graffiti in different European capitals. After moving to New York in 2008, he worked with many companies and brands, developing a reputation in graphic design and illustration for his distinctive style of translating complex ideas into simple and timeless visual stories.
He is also the owner and creative director of Hey Gee Studio, a full-service creative agency based in New York City.

Rae Burremo was a typical 5 year old when she developed leg pain that left her limping. For a couple weeks, her parents and doctors tried to figure out what was causing it until finally they looked at her legs with an MRI and she was diagnosed with Acute Lymphoblastic Leukemia. She had a great group of friends and family who supported her through treatment by making sure she always had her favorite salty snacks and plenty of art supplies. Rae loves spaghetti with red sauce, pepperoni pizza, and every kind of fruit. She is passionate about animals, is a devoted friend, and loves to listen to music, draw, jump on the trampoline, swim, figure skate and visit Disney World with her family. Rae is now a healthy 10-year-old in fourth grade who dreams of being an interior designer when she grows up.

ABOUT FONDATION IPSEN BOOKLAB

Fondation Ipsen improves the lives of millions of people around the world by rethinking scientific communication. The truthful transmission of science to the public is complex because scientific information is often technical and there is a lot of inaccurate information. In 2018, Fondation Ipsen established BookLab to address this need. BookLab books come about through collaboration between scientists, doctors, artists, authors, and children. In paper and electronic formats, and in several languages, BookLab delivers books across more than 50 countries for people of all ages and cultures. Fondation Ipsen BookLab's publications are free of charge to schools, libraries and people living in precarious situations. Join us! Access and share our books by visiting: www.fondation-ipsen.org.

ABOUT MAYO CLINIC PRESS

Launched in 2019, Mayo Clinic Press shines a light on the most fascinating stories in medicine and empowers individuals with the knowledge to build healthier, happier lives. From the award-winning *Mayo Clinic Health Letter* to books and media covering the scope of human health and wellness, Mayo Clinic Press publications provide readers with reliable and trusted content by some of the world's leading health care professionals. Proceeds benefit important medical research and education at Mayo Clinic. For more information about Mayo Clinic Press, visit mcpress.mayoclinic.org.

ABOUT THE COLLABORATION

The My Life Beyond series was developed in partnership between Fondation Ipsen's BookLab and Mayo Clinic, which has provided world-class medical education for more than 150 years. This collaboration aims to provide trustworthy, impactful resources for understanding childhood diseases and other problems that can affect children's well-being.

The series offers readers a holistic perspective of children's lives with — and beyond — their medical challenges. In creating these books, young people who have been Mayo Clinic patients worked together with author-illustrator Hey Gee, sharing their personal experiences. The resulting fictionalized stories authentically bring to life the patients' emotions and their inspiring responses to challenging circumstances. In addition, Mayo Clinic physicians contributed the latest medical expertise on each topic so that these stories can best help other patients, families and caregivers understand how children perceive and work through their own challenges.

Text: Hey Gee and Rae Burremo
Illustrations: Hey Gee

Medical editor: Mira A. Kohorst, M.D., Consultant, Department of Pediatric Hematology and Oncology,
Mayo Clinic, Rochester, MN; Assistant Professor of Pediatric Hematology and Oncology,
Mayo Clinic College of Medicine and Science

Managing editor: Anna Cavallo, Health Education and Content Services/Mayo Clinic Press, Mayo Clinic, Rochester, MN
Project manager: Kim Chandler, Department of Education, Mayo Clinic, Rochester, MN
Manager of publications: Céline Colombier-Maffre, Fondation Ipsen, Paris, France
President: James A. Levine, M.D., Ph.D., Professor, Fondation Ipsen, Paris, France

MAYO CLINIC PRESS
200 First St. SW
Rochester, MN 55905
mcpress.mayoclinic.org

The information in this book is true and complete to the best of our knowledge. This book is intended only as an
informative guide for those wishing to learn more about health issues. It is not intended to replace, countermand or
conflict with advice given to you by your own physician. The ultimate decision concerning your care should be made
between you and your doctor. Information in this book is offered with no guarantees. The author and publisher disclaim
all liability in connection with the use of this book.

For bulk sales to employers, member groups and health-related companies, contact Mayo Clinic, 200 First St. SW,
Rochester, MN 55905, or send an email to SpecialSalesMayoBooks@mayo.edu.

Proceeds from the sale of every book benefit important medical research and education at Mayo Clinic.

ISBN 978-1-893005-78-5

Library of Congress Control Number 2021943747

Printed in the United States of America